THE PHONY GOURMET

Also by the Authors

Sidetracked Home Executives

The Sidetracked Sisters Catch-up on the Kitchen

The Sidetracked Sisters' Happiness File

Get Your Act Together!

•Includes 75 Delicious Recipes for Shortcut Cooking•

THE PHONY GOURMET

PAM YOUNG
AND PEGGY JONES

Illustrated by Jim Shinn

HarperCollins*Publishers*

FIRST EDITION

Designed by Jessica Shatan

Library of Congress Cataloging-in-Publication Data

Young, Pam (Pamela I.)
The phony gourmet : includes 75 delicious recipes for shortcut cooking /
Pam Young and Peggy Jones ; illustrated by Jim Shinn. — 1st ed.
p.   cm.
Includes index.
ISBN 0-06-017204-5
1. Quick and easy cookery. 2. Kitchens I. Jones,
Peggy (Peggy A.) II. Title.
TX833.5.Y67   1995
641.5'55—dc20   95-78

95 96 97 98 99 ❖/HC 10 9 8 7 6 5 4 3 2 1

*This book is dedicated to
everyone who loves good food and to
the people who fix that food and get it on the table*

CONTENTS

ACKNOWLEDGMENTS

We want to thank our agent, John Boswell, for his fun-loving approach to work. If it were not for John, we would still be sitting on *The Phony Gourmet*.

We also want to thank our editor at HarperCollins, Nancy Peske, who guided us in the right direction by confiding what she didn't know about cooking. Having her come to one of our homes for dinner was the best possible mix of business and pleasure (and she never knew what she was eating).

We give special thanks to our genius editor/son/nephew, Jeffrey Jones, who did a fabulous job editing. Actually, Nancy Peske should thank him, too, because without his editing, she would have received a manuscript that would have put her in a cage.

After we twisted the arm he doesn't draw with, Jim Shinn agreed to do the illustrations in this book. His sense of humor shines in every drawing. Since he is a full-time illustrator for our local newspaper, *The Columbian,* we truly appreciate that he took his valuable free time to illustrate our book.

Special thanks to Brian Peters, who computed the instructions for the Pepperoni A-Frame Log Cabin into pictures.

Thanks also to our friends and relatives who shared their serious recipes with us, knowing they'd be converted into something different by a twist of the Phony Gourmet.

We thank Mom and Dad for letting us play in the kitchen when we were little.

We thank our kids Michael, Peggy, Joanna, Chris, Jeff, and Ally for eating what we fed them. We also owe particular thanks to our wonderful husbands, Danny and Terry, who leave us free to play with our work, and when our work is just plain work, they make dinner and do the dishes!

INTRODUCTION

It's kind of funny that the word *phony* is in the title of this cookbook because, honestly, it's about cooking in the real world. You probably wouldn't buy a book called *The Real Gourmet* because you'd think it was just another volume from some fancy chef whose collection of recipes would leave your sink full of dishes, your counters covered with chopping boards, mixing bowls, and gizmos, and a range top buried under pots and pans full of fancy-sounding concoctions.

We doubt that many "gourmet chefs" have spent twenty-seven years stuck in the same 8 × 10-foot ranch-style kitchen, cooking for the exact same people day in and day out, 365 days a year, year in and year out! We on the other side of the stove have done just that, and our voluntary confinement over the decades has given us valuable experience and time to create recipes that are quick, easy, and delicious, and because of our motto, "It's not WHAT you do, it's what they THINK you do," our recipes are very sneaky shortcuts—and that's where the word *phony* comes in.

What's Been Cooking at Your House?

The consumption of Big Macs is growing about as fast as the national debt. Almost seventy billion dollars is spent in fast-food restaurants annually, which tells us that meal preparation is not going too well in the average home.

As authors and public speakers, we travel all over the United States in an effort to help people simplify their home lives. We come in contact with thousands of people every year (mostly women), and when we ask an audience if they have meal preparation under control and organized, only about one percent raise their hands. Still, everyone looks well, if not over, fed.

We're all eating something, somewhere!

It is amazing to us that fancy cookbooks are so popular today when no one has time to cook. We buy the books, watch cooking shows, and clip out of magazines recipes with yummy pictures of the finished works, but we routinely end up commuting through morning traffic with an Egg McMuffin, grabbing a bite at Arby's for lunch, scarfing down a doughnut at a 7-Eleven for a snack, and scooping up take-out at Skippers for dinner. We don't make the recipes in the glossy cookbooks. We don't cook the entrées we watch being so meticulously prepared on television. We WISH we could and HOPE we will someday, but we rarely do, because WE DON'T HAVE THE TIME.

Reading the cookbooks, saving the recipes in magazines, clipping newspaper food columns, and watching the cooking shows are really more like hobbies or going to the movies. They provide us with an escape into a world of fine dining we'll probably never know. They play on our imaginations and they make us feel good by giving us hope for the possibility that someday we will do it all.

Let's all step out of denial and admit that for most of us time spent in the kitchen is minimal and we don't feel very good when we're in there. If you'd rather go in for a Pap smear and mammogram than frazzle up something for dinner, you will love the recipes in *The Phony Gourmet* cookbook.

Many of the recipes use brand-name convenience foods disguised to look home-made and are intended to fool those eating the food into thinking that the cook spent hours in the kitchen. False-labor recipes like Fraudulent Lasagna, Snickers Under a Blanket, and Aunt Peg's Five-Bean Summit Meeting are especially good for impressing company. Many of the frozen entrées in your grocer's freezer case are good just as they are, but when you taste our rip-off sauces or counterfeit crumb topping over some of these products you'll be excited to share the pirated meals with your friends and family.

We don't know the exact day the Phony Gourmet was born, but we do know that in the middle of the week in March of 1978, there was a twinkle in our eyes. At that time we were young mothers who had written a book on how to get organized. The popularity of the book led to an opportunity to appear regularly on a live television show in Portland, Oregon. We were in the trenches of motherhood with six kids (three each) between the ages of one and twelve. Monthly, we would emerge from our home fires with a creative gem for other mothers in similar predicaments.

One spring day we were creating together at one of our houses while some daytime-television talk show was yakking in the background. We weren't really paying that much attention, but out of the side of our ears we heard the announcer say, "COMING UP NEXT . . . WHAT TO DO WHEN HUBBY SAYS HE'S BRINGING THE BOSS HOME FOR DINNER IN HALF AN HOUR! . . . AND WE'LL BE RIGHT BACK."

After a commercial the huckster came back on with an aproned expert standing next to him. They were behind a long counter laden with quickie solutions.

We stopped what we were doing and waited to hear the words of wisdom we had been promised.

"The menu is," she croaked, "lamb chops, fresh asparagus with Hollandaise sauce, potato pompoms with Farquar and dill, and a crisp garden salad with raspberry vinaigrette dressing." We'd had our share of impromptu company dinners, but we'd never been able to go to the refrigerator or pantry and pull out that kind of stuff. . . . That's not crisis cooking, that's cooking for a king! We gave each other "the look" and then we heard her say that the dessert was an "elegant chocolate-almond torte." That did it! Before that, we were sort of tracking the scent of a great meal, but when she went over the falls with the dessert she lost us. We were on the floor in hysterics . . . and the Phony Gourmet was conceived.

So if you like the sound of Hungry Man in a Blanket, Savory Couch Potato Stew, Twice-Baked Bread, and Mousse in Almost a Minute, you'll love this collection of recipes that are hasty, tasty, and often very sneaky.

Before we move on to the real food for thought in this book, we would like to introduce you to the members of our families, who will be referred to frequently because they have been our guinea pigs in this lifelong experiment in creative food preparation. Peggy's husband is Danny and their children are Chris, Jeff, and Allyson. Pam's husband is Terry and their children are from previous marriages. Pam's children are Michael, Peggy Ann, and Joanna, and Terry's are Kristi and Eric.

It's our desire that the recipes in this book will please your family and friends as much as they have pleased ours. From the first recipe you try you'll need to start getting used to receiving compliments for minimal effort. Remembering it's not WHAT you do, it's what they THINK you do, it's important (if you want to be a real phony gourmet) to accept the compliments without giving away your secrets. If you can do that, you are ready to become a Phony Gourmet.

THE PHONY GOURMET

THE PHONY WAY

Home is where the heart is, and the hearts of our homes beat most strongly in our kitchens. There, we've shared our best stories, our most embarrassing moments, our beyondest dreams, and our deepest concerns. We've laughed, cried, and fought in that room. Gathering in the kitchen, we've dealt with each other's disappointments and insecurities and, best of all, we've experienced unconditional love.

We think about that a lot. Alone in our cozy old kitchens, we love sipping nice hot cups of tea, looking back on decades of cooking and feeling good. With all of our kids away, these once bustling sculleries are practically ghost kitchens, but it won't be that way for long. Wonderful warm kitchens will always draw people home for the holidays and other special occasions, and instinctively everyone always ends up in the kitchen.

Gathered around the kitchen table, sitting on the counter where the cupboards come together in the corner making a great backrest, leaning against the refrigerator, lying on the floor teasing the cat, looking in the pantry for dog treats or people snacks, circling, milling, hovering, or just passing through and pausing to catch the gist of what's going on ... everybody knows that people in the know stay close to the kitchen.

We are at a place in our lives where we realize that slaving over a hot stove is absurd. Our homemade happiness comes from being able to whip up delicious meals that are quick and simple. The meals are homemade and the happiness comes from the luxury of relaxing with the family and having time to listen instead of fuss. We have extra meals in the freezer to serve so that we're free to go play without worrying about dinner. Homemade happiness doesn't come from doing things perfectly, but from having a perfectly glorious time just being with the ones you love. From our kitchens to yours, we wish you simply delicious meals that your family will never forget.

What's So Phony?

"Nothing is either genuine or phony, but thinking makes it so."
—THE PHONY GOURMET

Who Is the Phony Gourmet?

The Phony Gourmet is anyone who loves to eat delicious food but doesn't have the time or inclination to spend a major part of his or her life in the kitchen.

The Phony Gourmet is one who appreciates dining out at an exquisite restaurant for a "culinary experience," but salivates when a McDonald's commercial comes on television. Most important, the Phony Gourmet is anyone who isn't quite ready to come out of the pantry with the truth and admit to the consistent and heavy use of convenience foods and routine fast-food patronage.

On a more serious note, the Phony Gourmet craves love and appreciation, wants hope and encouragement, needs rewards for doing well and forgiveness when something goes wrong. He or she has a dream . . . a purpose for living beyond slaving over a hot stove. The Phony Gourmet wants to have time to rest, play, be with the children, the spouse, and friends.

The Phony Gourmet wants excitement in life, yet peace in a home that is an oasis from the world, with romance bursting at the seams. He or she wants to eat right, exercise regularly, travel the world, dress for success, floss, invest, and recycle.

In summary, the Phony Gourmet wants to HAVE and DO it all! Unfortunately, there is only one Martha Stewart and most of us don't have a staff to pull off the stuff she comes up with. She grows her own orchids, makes her own draperies, looms her own cloth, stencils borders on her walls, publishes her own magazine, beds and breakfasts notables, and even lays carpet. She has a wine cellar, a walk-in china closet, a greenhouse, and probably a wildlife center where she hunts her own game. She is very busy. Her books sell extremely well because there is something in all of us that likes to see how much one person can do. For a split second we think that maybe we could do it too, even though we know we don't have the time or the energy, let alone the staff.

What Is a Gourmet . . . Really?

A gourmet is a connoisseur of food and drink and, according to Webster, a connoisseur is "one who enjoys with discrimination and appreciates subtleties."

Recently, we watched one of the great chefs on a cooking show, and she could tell the differences among garlic that had been minced with a French knife, pressed in a garlic press and, "God forbid," garlic powder. She winced at that thought. Her sense of taste was as refined as a hound's sense of smell.

We have a basset hound in the family who, every morning, lets her nose take her all over, as if her yard were the morning newspaper. Every few feet she stops to read the fine print, and often rereads sections of especially juicy gossip, appreciating the subtleties only a hound can relish. It's a joy to watch genius in action, whether it's in a chef or in a dog. But, it's folly for most of us to think that we could ever come close to discerning the difference between minced, pressed, or powdered garlic in a spaghetti sauce any more than we could expect someday to be able to wake up and smell the front porch and know who came by in the night.

The sense of smell is closely linked to what we can taste, and therefore to our ability to be connoisseurs of anything we put in our mouths. Recently we both temporarily lost our sense of smell, due to a debilitating sinus infection that left us impotent from the neck up. We learned from that experience that without a sense of smell our tongues were left on their own to convey just exactly what they had lying on them. Orphaned, a tongue can only tell that something is salty, sweet, sour, or bitter. Give a tongue a roll of LifeSavers, and if it is working alone without the nose, it will not be able to suck and tell the subtleties of the different flavors.

Judging by the glut of decongestants we discovered in the drugstore during our affliction, we bet that a lot of olfactory organs in America are on medication and that their owners can barely tell the difference between fresh lobster and road kill.

And what about the average sinus passage that's drug-free? Judging by the billions of dollars spent in fast-food restaurants, it's our guess that if you blindfolded those of us with healthy sinus cavities, the only connoisseuring going on would be a rather sophisticated ability to discriminate between the distinctive greases in the air put out by Burger King, Taco Bell, McDonald's, KFC, Wendy's, Burgerville (well, you'd have to come to the northwest for that one), and the list could go on forever.

SO LET'S GET REALISTIC! Remember the story of the Emperor's New Clothes? He wanted a new suit for the big parade, and two wandering shyster tailors came along and talked him into invisible fabric. They told him that the material was so exquisite that only well-bred royalty could see it. The emperor, evidently shaky about his breeding and royal status, wouldn't admit that he couldn't see the invisible bolt and ended up exposing his insecurities to the whole kingdom.

There's a little bit of the emperor in all of us. We've gotten snagged into grinding our own coffee beans for a perfect cup of coffee, yet we'll turn around and rave over a cup of Taster's Choice when we don't know that's what it is. We like the idea of wine-tasting, but even the best in that field can get tripped. In fact, we saw a world-renowned wine connoisseur fail a test on *The Today Show.* Blindfolded, he picked the cheapest wine as the best and he DIDN'T work for some cheap wine company like The Three Muscatels.

We can control the emperor in us if every time we're tempted to search out fresh coriander leaves, or track down goose pâté, we just remind ourselves of our last visit to Wendy's. If it was within the last week, we need to tune out the gourmets and open a can of Campbell's. Besides helping you to put the emperor behind you and getting you to be honest about this whole eating thing, we want this book to dissolve the gourmet mystique and dissipate the smoke screen that has been wafting over the masses for centuries. We need to unite as common eaters and see the truth behind the stuck-up, snooty, stuffy, and often pompous chef complexes that lurk in most of the gourmet cookbooks, seep from the kitchens of four-star hotels, and drip from the lips of some of the TV gourmets.

Let's start with some thought about what those "experts" learn to do before they feed us.

Six Secret Lessons from the Culinary Arts Industry

Remember that the master chefs SPEND MOST OF THEIR LIVES IN THEIR KITCHENS, so we want to be careful that what they have to tell us doesn't lead us into their way of life. What we CAN learn from them are their SIX SECRETS.

Several years ago, we spent a day in Los Angeles at a very famous cooking school.

On this particular day, the teachers and students weren't around so we don't really know what they teach there, but we can guess that there are probably six main lessons: 1. DENIAL, 2. TITLING, 3. ATTITUDINAL PRESENTATION, 4. EAT HALF, SERVE HALF, 5. COVER UP, and 6. LEFTOVERS.

Of course, these lessons are top secret and no regular person will EVER get hold of this classified information. We can only hazard a presumption of what goes on behind the sequestering doors of the great cooking schools.

SECRET LESSON 1: DENIAL

The first thing we think they must teach is that when you make a mistake, DENY it. If, when you serve the "mistake," you maintain a godlike attitude, you'll be able to get the people to eat almost anything. How do you think they've been able to get us "common folk" to order things like "blackened cod"? The chef who pulled that one off was not about to admit that he'd been talking to his girlfriend on the phone and burned his fish. He simply sent the charred piece of cod out on a platter of parsley and called it "blackened." No apology. No explanation. At home, if you took a plate of burned fish to the table, everybody would feel sorry for you and you'd all head out for Long John Silver's. But a chef can get away with it. He'd never dream of coming out of the kitchen to say, "Hey, here's the deal, my girlfriend broke up with me and I burned your fish—can you eat it black, 'cause it's still good on the inside, or do you want me to try again as soon as I've stopped crying?" Now, we, the intimidated public, actually order our fish burned.

Because of self-saturated chefs who have had the audacity to DENY that they made a mistake, there are other foods with which we are very familiar. Sour cream and blue cheese . . . cream accidentally left out at room temperature by stupid chefs. Wine . . . grape juice left in the cellar by a reclusive chef. Raw oysters, sushi, and cold soups came into vogue when the stove didn't get turned on and the hungry patrons were getting cranky. Wilted lettuce salad? Go figure. Our guess is old produce.

SECRET LESSON 2: TITLING

In addition to denial, one can always add a fancy name to a mistake. There are many food foul-ups that have been accepted by an adoring public just because of the NAMES given to them. Bananas flambé and cherries jubilee are perfect examples. They were originally the results of culinary tosspots chugging brandy, setting the fruit on fire, and serving it with a festive or French name.

The first omelet was supposed to be called a soufflé, but the 400-pound chef fell in the kitchen, and so did the intended fluff of the eggs.

The first quiche was really supposed to be a custard pie, but the scatter-brained chef forgot to order sugar, so he added ham and onion instead and named it quiche.

Chicken Marengo is a very famous French dish that was concocted on the spot by Napoleon's chef after the battle of Marengo. He used what he had on hand, and since there was a big war going on, there was not enough chicken to make a chicken dish (we wonder what chickens do during wartime), so he threw in crayfish tails, fried eggs, mushrooms, and truffles (underground mushrooms that trained pigs find and dig up). You'll be safe, in the future, to add the name "Marengo" to any dish you have put together on the spot because you haven't had time to go to the store, or if there's a war going on in your home.

It wouldn't hurt to memorize a few French cooking terms, or make up your own. If you took ballet, you already have an army of terms you can convert to titles for food. Here are a few to get you started:

Pork Grand Battement
Fish Fouetté
Shrimp Glissade
Potato Jeté
Chicken Entrechat
Eggs Pas de Deux
Mushroom Relevé
Rond de Jambe de Lamb
Pasta Plié
Beef Arabesque

Don't forget, Marengo.

It's important to note that, throughout this cookbook, whenever we use a foreign word we will translate it in parentheses, not because we don't think you know what it means, but because we just found out ourselves. We have an inkling that if we don't know a word, many of you might not either. Take pride and give yourself points for any or all of the definitions and translations that you do know.

SECRET LESSON 3:
ATTITUDINAL PRESENTATION

It isn't a secret that most chefs have an attitude. We have always been just a little intimidated by gourmet chefs because many of them seem to have a superiority complex. We blame that, too, on the culinary arts industry. We think most chefs are intimidating because they learned to be that way at school. (When a Pillsbury Dough Boy hat is put on the head of a guy who has a certificate showing he has graduated from a cooking school, he can get as cocky as if he's just been graduated from law school or been awarded his doctorate.) To serve a culinary mistake with pride takes ego, education, the hat, and probably the fear that comes with knowing that the owner of the restaurant could take the price of any wrecked food out of one's paycheck.

From now on, regardless of what happens in the kitchen, remember attitudinal presentation! If you burn it or ruin it in some other way, serve it anyway, with confidence. If you run out of something, even if it's a main ingredient, substitute something else, name it with an ATTITUDE, and NEVER apologize! By naming it and acting as if it wasn't a mistake, you'll be able to pull off anything that happens from this point on, and you may even become famous for it some day. In keeping with the appropriate attitude, attribute any criticism from your eaters to a primitive palate.

SECRET LESSON 4:
EAT HALF, SERVE HALF

This lesson is self-explanatory and requires little commentary. Have you ever noticed how small the entrée portions are in fancy restaurants? Think about it. How many thin chefs do you know? A few months ago, we had to stay in Manhattan for a week at a hotel with a restaurant that had a four-star rating. On the fifth evening of our stay, we were so sick of premature vegetables and the chef's teeny-weeny entrées bedded in designer greens or submerged in fancy foreign sauces that we took a cab to Times Square where we know the Marriott serves recognizable meals. We got to order baked potatoes . . . and they let us have sour cream, butter, and chives without scoffing at our requests.

SECRET LESSON 5: COVER UP

Remember, "It's not what you do, it's what they think you do." We think chefs learn to cover up stuff they're not that happy with by using sauces, crusts, and toppings. As you know, those three items are always touted on menus, when really they could be hiding a legion of errors. What started out to be deceitful has ended up being something we value highly. We doubt that sauces are always used to enhance a food. More often than not, they are probably used to cover up old food, ugly food, or scary food like squid.

Whenever we hear the word *marinade,* we like it. But we wonder if sleazy chefs do a lot of behind-closed-doors marinating in an effort to preserve meats and keep them digestible for a few days longer.

We may be wrong, but we think crusts are a big cover-up too. Crust seems like a big deal because we're all scared of rolling pins. Whenever something is "en croûte" (in a crust), be careful. The question is, what's under the croûte?

SECRET LESSON 6: LEFTOVERS

We're almost positive that chefs do NOT view leftovers as leftovers. We believe that they think of them more like building blocks for tomorrow. When the soup de jour (soup of the day) is still there tomorrow, we're sure they don't try to serve it again as soup. Have you ever seen on a menu soup d'hier (soup from yesterday)? No. That's because most chefs have learned to take the soup d'hier and turn it into a sauce de jour, because they know that in most cases something that was good today will be even better tomorrow.

Chefs learn to take advantage of the whatevers from yesterday, put them to use, and concoct fabulous dishes for today. Leftovers should never be served again in the same way they were served the first time. There are a few exceptions like spaghetti, potato salad, roast beef, and some of those foods you like knowing are in the refrigerator when you go to bed. Unfortunately, those thoughts can wake you up in the middle of the night because of a subconscious fear that somebody will get to them tomorrow before you do.

Now that you know the six secrets of the elite at the top of the restaurant food chain, there's a little more to learn from the fellows lower down the chain.

Taking the Fast-Food Industry into Your Own Home

From Pam

For seven years, my former husband and I were in the fast-food restaurant business. We should all be attempting to create that industry in our own kitchens, because we don't have time to fix the foods our fore-mothers prepared.

It occurred to me that if I could bring the principles used in the fast-food indus-try into my meal preparation, I would spend less time in the kitchen and more time enjoying my family. It's true, and it has saved me vacations of time over the years. There are shortcuts and time-savers used by the fast-food industry that will cut your time in the kitchen to shreds, and though the recipes in this book are quick and easy, you'll even be able to cut down our times.

Usually, when we think of fast food, we think of grease, but there is an abundance of wisdom behind that grease. I know, because we had a twenty-four-hour restau-rant that served a full menu: breakfast, lunch, dinner, and desserts. We had a prep cook who would come in and precook items for the next shift, like bacon and sausage. He would also chop a shift's worth of onions, celery, tomatoes, olives, peppers, cabbage, mushrooms, carrots, and so on. He made sure there were hard-boiled eggs, thawed steaks, chicken, and fish. He'd cook huge pots of pasta and potatoes, slice meats, and fill containers so that the fast-food cook could put out his/her food within six or seven minutes of the order. If you spend a little time think-ing like a prep cook, you can save yourself hours of time when it comes to that crucial hour when everybody in the house starts to swarm into the kitchen like hornets around a mud hole.

There are three rules to running a suc-cessful fast-food operation in your home:

1. Buy and prepare in bulk. Freeze.
2. Whenever possible, add fresh ingredi-ents to whatever was canned, dehydrated or frozen. Use the list of ingredients on the label as a guide.
3. Serve piping hot, frozen solid, or chilled thoroughly.

To be your own fast-food prep cook, you'll need a zillion reclosable freezer bags (quart and gallon size), labels, a food processor, and a freezer.

FAST-FOOD TIPS

- If you have to make a mess anyway, you may as well make more for your mess. Frying bacon is messy, so when a recipe calls for half a pound of bacon, fry the whole pound and freeze the other half.
- When you get the food processor out to chop up an onion, chop a week's supply and store in a reclosable freezer bag in the refrigerator. Even after a week, the onions will still be good to use for cooking.
- When you get out a big pot to boil pasta, boil three times as much as you need and freeze two-thirds of it in reclosable freezer bags.
- When you fire up the barbecue to cook one chicken, you may as well barbecue three and freeze two, because cooked chicken freezes very well and the barbecue taste goes right along with it.

Setting Up the Phony Gourmet Kitchen

In the last five years, we have been invited into forty-five homes from New York to Sacramento to inspect the kitchens in an effort to streamline and reorganize them. In every kitchen we found too much stuff. If you want to put out quick, easy, and delicious meals, you need an efficient and streamlined place in which to do it.

Start by taking an inventory of your kitchen. Take an inventory of your kitchen. We repeat because it will help you to realize that you, too, have too much in it. Look at your kitchen with new eyes. If you see anything that you haven't used in over a year, get rid of it. The best way to clean out a pantry is to gut it, wash the shelves, and keep just what you will really use. You will need to do this with your cupboards and drawers too. Once we have gutted a drawer, our motto is: Think before you fill your drawers! Remember, you are going to need room for the staples you are really going to use.

SPICES

In the forty-five homes we went into, universally we found spices that were no longer doing what their name implied. We decided that the average cook needs to do what we call the SNIFF, PRICE AND SHAKE test on the stash of those little jars and cans in the cupboard.

1. If it smells like old hay, dump it.
2. If the price is under a dollar, pitch it.
3. If the contents won't shake, give it up.

KNIVES

Get good knives AND a knife sharpener. Your knives definitely need to be the best. When you buy good knives and take care of them, which means never putting them through the dishwasher, you will have them for a lifetime. To work at peak efficiency in the kitchen, you will need the following knives:

French knife
Boning knife
Paring knife
Bread knife
Steak knives (6 to 8)

IN THE KNIFE FAMILY
Potato peeler
Kitchen scissors
Egg slicer
Cheese slicer

APPLIANCES

Food Processor
There are many food processors on the market. We both happen to have Cuisinarts and we love them. (Remember, we do not get paid by Mr. Cuisinart.) If you don't have a food processor, you should really consider getting one. They are expensive, but you deserve one. Chopping, cutting, julienning, shredding, or grinding by hand is like going out in the backyard to go to the bathroom.

A food processor will chop vegetables finely or coarsely, depending on how long the machine is turned on. One quick on-off motion will leave a carrot in pieces about the size of AA batteries. Two or three on-off movements and the vegetable will be reduced to pieces the size of cooked rice. The machine left in the "on" position will turn the carrot into a bright orange pulp.

A food processor can grind meat, grate cheese, make bread crumbs, mix pastry dough, and smooth out gravies and sauces. Any leftover pasta or potato dishes can be puréed and frozen to use for thickening soups or adding to casseroles as you see fit. Just be sure to LABEL whatever dish you puréed, so that you can know what's in the bag.

Other Appliances
Crockery cooker (large, with a submersible crock)
Freezer
Refrigerator
Microwave
Hand mixer
Blender

UTENSILS
Can opener
Garlic press
Colander
Measuring spoons
Measuring cups (1 quart, 1 cup, ¾ cup,
    ⅔ cup, ½ cup, ⅓ cup, ¼ cup)
Tongs (2 pairs)
Slotted spoons
Ladle
Mixing bowls (small, medium, large, and
    huge)
Mixing spoons
Lemon juicer
Strainers (small and large)

POTS AND PANS
You deserve good cookware. We recommend Calphalon. It is expensive, but it's worth the extra investment. In our experience we've had many different brands of cookware. The cheap stuff is thin and flimsy and food burns easily. The copper-bottom pots and pans require almost as much cleaning and polishing as cooking time. Calphalon is thick like Grandma's old iron frying pan, but it's not heavy. Food cooks evenly and nothing sticks, so cleanup is easy. Calphalon is also dishwasher safe.

Skillets
small (about an 8-inch diameter bottom
    with enough room for a slice of sand-
    wich bread or two cups of water)
medium (about a 10-inch diameter bottom
    with enough room for a slice of sand-
    wich bread or 3 cups of water)
large (about a 12-inch diameter bottom
    with enough room for two slices of
    sandwich bread, 5 cups of water, and a
    partridge in a pear tree)

Saucepans (with lids)
1 small (1-quart)
1 medium (2-quart)
1 large (3-quart)

Soup Pots (with lids)
1 20-quart
1 12-quart
1 6-quart

Roasting Pan (with lid)

Large Dutch Oven (3-quart)

BAKING DISHES AND PANS
Pyrex is great. It's inexpensive and it will go in the oven, microwave, and dishwasher. It comes in all shapes and some pieces

come with baskets that make it easy to serve from oven to table.

Pie plates
1 9-inch
1 10-inch
1 11-inch

Casseroles (with lids)
1½-quart
2-quart

THE PHONY PANTRY

Before we go any further, we need to seriously address the subject of convenience foods. It seems that whenever you hear the words *convenience food,* you tend to wince and think of something bad. The only reason that happens in your brain is because many of the products taste like wallpaper paste, at best. But let's not throw the wallpaper out with the paste. Convenience foods save time, but that should not be the REAL reason you use them.

Today, there are many exceptional products on the market that we suggest using in our recipes. In fact, this book could look like a running commercial for the folks at Swanson, Stouffer's, Campbell's, Lawry's, Pepperidge Farm, Knorr, and others. It's important to us that you know we are not receiving any money for recommending these fantastic products. We took the time to name them specifically because we want you to serve the very best. If you have

your own favorites, be sure to honor your own tastes over ours. Any reference to specific brands comes straight from our grateful hearts and decades of using these quality products to feed our families. We have been using some of these products for so long that we no longer consider them CONVENIENCE FOODS, but rather STAPLES.

Over the years, the definition of convenience food has changed. In our great-grandmothers' time, flour, butter, sugar, and cheese (that could all be purchased in the general store), were considered CONVENIENCE FOODS, and probably the die-hard pioneers thumbed the new-agers who didn't grow their own wheat, mill their own flour, or milk their own cows.

By the time our grandmothers took over the kitchens, flour, milk, and butter were no longer considered CONVENIENCE FOODS, but had become STAPLES. Store-bought bread was a convenience food. Today we don't think of bread as a convenience food, it's a STAPLE. The only people left baking all their own bread (without machines) these days are the Amish, and we read in a library book that they have a high suicide rate. Thank goodness the convenience food industry has prevailed!

Aside from wanting to clear the culinary smoke screen and convince you that there are wonderful products in stores today, we want you to have fun in the kitchen. When we were young, most of us were told not to play with our food. We need to unlearn that admonition: Start experimenting. Don't be afraid to use your right brain when you're in the kitchen. So what if once in a while you end up with something that tastes like Joe Montana's socks. Just put a nice sauce over it and serve it with pride. (Remember, too, the dog loves you and he'll always eat anything you serve!)

In order to be purists, as far as the Phony Gourmet is concerned, all of our recipes call for the simplest and fastest ingredients. In the following pages, we have given you the alternatives we use, when and if we have the time and/or energy. You can decide for yourself whether or not you will add more work to your already busy schedule. It's all up to you. Most of us don't have time to mince, julienne (make long, thin strips of vegetables and meat), stir constantly, measure a bunch of quarter teaspoons of unfamiliar spices, or make much of anything from scratch. Yet most cookbooks assume we do. Peggy read in a cookbook that one should ALWAYS use fresh chicken and beef stock when cooking, and only in an extreme EMERGENCY may one resort to using canned chicken or beef stock, but NEVER (yes, it was all capped), NEVER use bouillon cubes.

Ring, ring, ring.
"Hello?"
"Sissy, did you know you're not EVER supposed to use bouillon cubes?"
"No, did you?"
"No, I use 'em all the time and nobody's ever complained."
"Yeah, but look at the group you're serving."
"Huh?"
"Well, I mean Danny and the kids aren't exactly dignitaries eating at the White House."
"Do you use 'em?"
"Dignitaries?"
"No, bouillon cubes."
"Yeah, if I've run out of my own chicken

stock. You know how I love to make it myself."

"Can Terry tell?"

"That I love to make it myself?"

"No, can he tell when you've used bouillon cubes?"

"Are you kidding? He wouldn't know the difference between a bouillon cube and a dog food kibble, as long as it was dissolved and sorta warm."

"Right. You know that cookbook made me feel so cheap and stupid. Like bouillon cubes are death in a square."

"Well, they're not and we'd be stupid not to use them when we need to."

Whenever you do have a little extra time, it's always best to use fresh ingredients and there is no argument that made-from-scratch recipes are great (if you are a good cook), but when you're pressed for time, go for the bouillon cubes!

All About Beef Stock

Canned beef stock: Campbell's Beef Broth comes in a 10½-ounce can and makes 21 ounces of beef broth.

Beef bouillon cubes: One cube, dissolved in 1 cup of water, makes 1 cup of stock.

Beef food base: Gourmet Edge Beef

comes in a 16-ounce jar that needs to be refrigerated upon opening. Four teaspoons, mixed with 1 quart of water, make 1 quart of beef stock.

All About Chicken Stock

We have a recipe for HOMEMADE CHICKEN STOCK (see Index), but when a recipe calls for chicken stock, you have several VALID options. You can make HOMEMADE CHICKEN STOCK yourself, ONLY if you WANT to and you have the TIME.

Consider that if you make it from scratch, it's going to take at least a couple of hours, by the time you bone the chicken, fill and freeze the bags of chicken stock, and clean up. There is the wonderful aroma that comes from making chicken stock, and, if you have the time, you'll love our recipe, but that must be weighed against the amount of time you want and have to spend in the kitchen.

Canned chicken broth: Campbell's Chicken Broth comes in a 10½-ounce can. It makes 21 ounces of chicken stock.

Chicken bouillon cubes: One cube, dissolved in 1 cup of water, makes 1 cup of stock.

Chicken food base: Gourmet Edge

Chicken comes in a 16-ounce jar that needs to be refrigerated upon opening. Four teaspoons, mixed with 1 quart of water, make 1 quart of chicken stock.

All About Garlic

(a European bulbous herb of the lily family)

When our recipes call for garlic, we will either tell you to use powdered garlic, whole garlic, or garlic thinly sliced. You will notice that when a recipe calls for whole garlic, there will be a food processor or blender involved. That's because it's easier to toss the number of cloves needed into a blender with the other ingredients than it is to measure out a quantity of garlic powder. When a recipe calls for thinly sliced garlic, it will usually be a marinade recipe and the strength of fresh garlic is necessary.

Garlic powder: Lawry's Garlic Powder Coarse Ground with Parsley is an excellent product: ¼ teaspoon equals 1 medium clove.

Polander Crushed Garlic: This crushed garlic comes in a 4.5-ounce jar and is an excellent product: ½ teaspoon equals 1 clove. The jar contains approxi-mately 50 cloves and needs to be refrigerated once it is opened.

Fresh garlic: You can clean a bunch of bulbs of garlic and store the cloves in a tightly covered jar full of olive oil. The oil preserves the garlic for at least a month and is heavenly to use in cooking.

Pressed garlic: When you press a clove of garlic in a garlic press, all the juice and half the pulp comes out the holes. Take a sharp paring knife and scrape the pulp away from the holes. You can use the pulp that didn't go through the holes, if you have other pieces of vegetables like onions and celery in the recipe (such as stews and soups). You won't want to use the leftover pulp if you are making something like garlic butter, because you won't want hunks of pulp in the butter. Rule: If it's a sturdy dish, use the pulp, but if it's delicate, the pulp would offend.

Minced garlic: Place the clove of garlic on a cutting board. Lay the blade of a French knife on its side over the clove and give the knife blade a good smack, smashing the clove that's underneath. The hard skin will peel off easily. If you are right-handed, hold the point of the knife blade down on the cutting board with your left hand, mincing the garlic by moving the handle up and down with tiny chopping motions with your right hand. (If this isn't clear, go turn on a cable cooking show and you'll see it being done at this very minute.) Don't get cocky as a beginner, though. The audience claps because the cook is a showman. You don't need applause, you just need minced garlic.

All About Onions

(an Asian herb of the lily family with pungent, edible bulbs)

We've been eating onions for more than 4,000 years. Onions were part of the diet of the slaves who built the Pyramids in Egypt, which is not to say that serving more of them is going to get your family to help more around the house, but that they are nutritious and tasty. Thanks to world trade, we don't have to go any farther than our own gardens or supermarket to procure them.

Chopped onion: When a recipe calls for chopped onion, the pieces should be about the size of kidney beans. If you have a food processor, chop a week's supply of onions and store in a gallon-size reclosable storage bag. These onions should only be used in cooking and marinating, not in salads. Onions should be cut fresh for salads.

Minced onion: When a recipe calls for minced onion, the pieces should be about the size of cooked rice. If you use a food processor you will process a little longer than you would to chop them.

Thinly sliced onion: When we say to slice an onion thinly, we want it sliced about ⅛ of an inch thick. Use whole circles (separated) of thinly sliced onions for salads and garnish. For recipes that require thin pieces of sliced onion, pretend a thin slice is the face of a clock and cut diagonally at ten-minute increments. What you don't want when you are eating is to have a long piece of transparent, wormlike cooked onion hang off your fork and stick to your chin when you try to maneuver it into your mouth. Nobody wants that.

In most of our recipes, we have called for fresh onion. However, there are excellent onion products on the market today that save you time, and taste just as good as fresh onions in cooking.

The following commercial onion products may be used in the preparation of appetizers and dips, soups and chowders, stews, all meats including game, fish, shellfish, poultry, salads and salad dressings, sauces, vegetables, gravies, stuffings, cheese dishes, egg dishes, breads, casseroles and rice dishes.

Onion powder: Use for flavor only. This product will not provide any texture. One tablespoon onion powder equals 1 medium raw onion.

Instant minced onion: This product will provide flavor and texture. One table-spoon instant minced onion equals ¼ cup minced raw onion.

Instant chopped onion: This product will provide flavor and texture too. One-quarter cup chopped instant onions equals 1 cup chopped raw onion.

Onion flakes: This product will also provide flavor and texture. One tablespoon onion flakes equals ¼ cup chopped raw onion.

Onion juice: For flavor only. Use onion juice when a mild flavor of onion is desired. One to 2 teaspoons in ½ cup sour cream makes a great dip.

All About Potatoes

(an erect American edible tuber of the nightshade family)

How lucky we are to live in the last decade of the twentieth century. The bless-ing we say at our table before we put some-thing from the nightshade family into our mouths should include thanks to our ancestors who tested which tubers and bulbs were edible and which ones weren't.

"Father, bless those who went before us!"

Since we live in the state of Washington, we are neighbors to Idaho, the most famous state in America for the production of potatoes. Of course we only buy Idaho potatoes and of course we are highly influ-enced by our neighboring state's market-ing and advertising. No, we don't get paid by the state of Idaho for promoting these national treasures, we recommend them because Idaho potatoes are superior and we have been cooking with them since our first experiences in the kitchen.

There are several varieties of potatoes used in our recipes:

Baking potatoes: These potatoes are oval in shape and are a russet brown or dirt color. They are great for baking and are often referred to as "bakers." They are very good used in gratin recipes, for making hash browns, and for mashing. When we refer to different sizes of baking potatoes in our recipes, use these equivalent examples:

Large—About the size of an oval Big Mac
Medium—About the size of a lady's fist
   (unless the lady has eaten too many Big Macs and then we're back to large)

Small—Don't buy them in small (they represent a crop failure)

White new potatoes: These potatoes are excellent for making potato salad.

They are also wonderful in stews and soups, because they cook down into a smoother gravylike texture than their brown brother, the baker.

Equivalent examples are:

Large—About the size of a three-way light bulb
Medium—About the size of a 60-watt light bulb
Small—About the size of a night light (go ahead and buy the small size if you'd like; they represent youth)

Red potatoes: These potatoes are excellent when used in potato salads and are delicious in hot, German-style potato dishes. They are very good in stews and soups, but they make mashed potatoes that won't fluff. The very small red potatoes (about the size of a walnut) are easy to cook because no cutting is necessary. They're pretty, too.

Instant Potatoes: There are some excellent instant potato products on the market. OreIda frozen potato products are superb, and so are OreIda Instant Potatoes. Potato Buds, a General Mills product, are excellent too. Our kids were so used to instant that one Thanksgiving, when we mashed from scratch, one of them said, "What happened to the potatoes?" It wasn't a "better or worse" statement, just recognition that they were different.

All About Tomatoes

(a South American herb of the nightshade family, widely cultivated for its edible fruit)

Freeze all sizes of tomatoes straight from the vine (stems removed), in reclosable freezer bags. When you need tomatoes in top-of-the-stove cooking recipes, take the number you need from the freezer and put them in the skillet or pot. The skins will come off on their own and float to the top to be skimmed off as you see them.

You have probably seen television chefs carefully remove seeds from tomatoes. It's our guess they are concerned with an affliction called diverticulitis. A person with this problem has pockets in his or her intestinal tract where small particles like tomato and sesame seeds can get caught, inflame the area, and cause appendicitis-type pains. If this happens to you, perhaps you should check with your doctor before eating tomatoes, seeds and all. Otherwise, enjoy the whole fruit. The seeds are one of the best parts.

All About Spices

(an aromatic vegetable product used to season or flavor foods)

The terms *spice* and *spices* are often used in a general sense to mean any aromatic flavoring material of vegetable origin, of course, and are often used in a more specific sense, together with the terms *herb, seed,* and *condiment* as defined below. (Ho, hum . . . don't fall asleep yet. If you read the definitions they may serve you well, if you ever get to be on *Jeopardy!*) Again, our thanks must go to our ancestors who probably tested all aromatic vegetation on the planet, and either died, retched, hallucinated, or became paralyzed, addicted, or nourished.

Spices: Aromatic natural products, which are the dried seeds, buds, fruit or flower parts, bark, or roots of plants, usually of tropical origin. They can be found in tins or bottles and look nice in a designer rack.

Herbs: Aromatic leaves and sometimes the flowers of plants, usually of a temperate origin. Picked fresh from your own garden and hung upside down to dry; they are especially intimidating.

Seeds: Aromatic, dried, small whole fruits or seeds, usually of a temperate origin. Faith in the grain of one of these can move mountains. (Matthew 17:20)

Blend: A mixture of spices, herbs, seeds, or other flavoring materials, either ground or whole.

Condiment: A spice, herb, or seed; but more frequently a pungent, prepared mixture of seasonings sometimes in liquid form. Condiments in many forms may be served as an accompaniment to foods. Prepared mustards and catsup are condiments. Chutney is a scary condiment.

Well-seasoned food, very simply, is food that has been made to taste especially good without any predominating flavor. It is food that has been given a bit of flavor variety through the correct use of spices and herbs.

Tastes differ greatly. Therefore, it is very difficult to give exacting and precise directions for seasoning. What may send one person into a spiritual experience may cause another to empty a mouthful into a napkin when no one is looking. Remember in the movie *Big* when Tom Hanks scraped the caviar off his tongue? You don't want your guests to have to do that. The seasoning of food must vary to suit the tastes of those whom you are serving. One important rule to remember is that the seasonings should be used in small quantities, particularly a new flavor you are trying for the first time.

One may always add more if desired, but it is impossible to correct or remove seasoning if too much has been used initially. Seasonings of all kinds, as well as spices and herbs, should enhance the natural flavor, never overpower it. Of course, there will always be a few exceptions to any rule, as in the cases of dishes such as curry or chili.

Spices and herbs make it possible for you to serve food that has variety and is more appetizing in aroma, more appealing in color, tastier, and more digestible. Spice and herb cookery need not be complicated nor time-consuming nor expensive. It doesn't necessarily mean preparing and serving fancy, hot, exotic dishes, although you might find these to be fun to make occasionally.

Lawry's Seasoned Salt: A fabulous blend of salt, herbs, and spices. It adds flavor and excitement that ordinary salt cannot match. Shake it on all meats before and after cooking. It flavors soups, gravies, stews, and casseroles. Sprinkle it on salads, poultry, vegetables, and eggs. You will see it in the majority of our recipes. According to the label, Lawry's contains salt, sugar, spices including paprika and turmeric, onion, cornstarch, and garlic. It does NOT contain MSG.

All About Staples

If you follow our recipes and you don't already have your own favorites, BUY THESE STAPLES!

Bel-Air Frozen Stew Vegetables
Best Foods (Hellmann's) Dijonnaise
Best Foods (Hellmann's) Mayonnaise
B & M Brick Oven Baked Beans
Bull's-Eye Barbecue Sauce (Original)
Cajun's Choice Creole Seasoning
Campbell's Old Fashioned Baked Beans
Campbell's Soups
Classic Soups Tortellini Vegetable
    Stockpot Soup Concentrate
Dole Crushed Pineapple
Durkee Redhot Cayenne Pepper Sauce
Gerber Baby Food
Heinz Vegetarian Beans in Tomato Sauce
Hollandaise Sauce Blend from The
    McCormick Collection

Knorr Cream of Wild Mushroom Soupmix
Knorr Leek Soup
Knorr Pepper Sauce Mix
Knorr Pesto Sauce
Knorr Vegetarian Vegetable Bouillon Cubes
Kraft Free Mayonnaise
Lawry's Beef Marinade
Lawry's Brown Gravy Mix
Lawry's Carne Asada Marinade
Lawry's Garlic Powder Coarse Ground
    with Parsley
Lawry's Mesquite Marinade
Lawry's Seasoned Salt
Lawry's Southwest Chicken Marinade
Lea & Perrins Worcestershire Sauce
Lipton Soups
Molly McButter
OreIda Hash Browns
Pace Thick & Chunky Medium Salsa
Pam No Stick Cooking Spray (no relation)
Pepperidge Farm Puff Pastry Sheets
    (frozen)

Pepperidge Farm Puff Pastry Shells
    (frozen)
Philadelphia Brand Cream Cheese (this is
    definitely the smoothest)
Presti's Taco Seasoning
Progresso Bread Crumbs
Rosarita Refried Beans
Schilling Dill Weed
Schilling Meat Marinade
Stock Pot Soups
Stouffer's Lasagna with Meat &
    Sauce
Stouffer's Lean Cuisine
Swanson Hungry Man Frozen Dinners
S & W Premium Baked Beans with Brown
    Beans
Tillamook Cheddar Cheese (this is our
    favorite brand of Cheddar; if you have a
    favorite, use it)
Totino's Party Pizzas
Tyson Chicken
Van Camp's Pork and Beans

MORE SNEAKY TECHNIQUES

All About Room Deodorizers

Over the years we have discovered many ways to give the illusion that some serious cooking was happening when we really hadn't done anything but put something in the oven from a previous time. The old put-a-piece-of-bread-in-the-oven-when-you're-trying-to-sell-your-house tip is good, but it's not very sophisticated.

AROMA ONLY

On a day when you are really going to be cooking, don't throw away all of the stuff you usually do. Instead, save things like the fat trimmed from any meat, chicken skin and bones, onion skins and ends, garlic skins and ends, carrot and potato peelings, celery stumps, etc. Freeze them in a reclosable freezer bag. To use on those days when you will need to create the illusion of a pending meal by aroma, follow one of our two basic recipes for FALSE LABOR IN THE KITCHEN.

Aroma Only (Main Dish)

This will smell so good you might almost forget that it's a trick! Do not be tempted to open the foil; you'll embarrass yourself.

PREPARATION TIME: 2 minutes
COOKING TIME: 3 to 4 hours

½   cup Bisquick
1   cup water
1½ cups frozen garbage

1. In a mug, make paste with Bisquick and water.

2. Place garbage in center of a large piece of aluminum foil. Pour paste over garbage. Wrap and poke about 6 holes in the top of the foil.

3. Bake in a 300-degree oven until the aroma starts to waft. Reduce heat to 250 and waft for up to 4 hours.

4. Discard after scam is over.

Tip: By adding various spices, you can make the house smell like Mexico, Italy, China, Germany, or wherever you'd like to go.

Aroma Only (Dessert)

In order to counterfeit the smell of dessert, there are a few changes that need to be made to AROMA ONLY (MAIN DISH).

1. Use fruit peelings of any kind: orange, apple, pineapple, pear, or others instead of vegetable and meat trimmings.

2. Add to paste 1 teaspoon each cinnamon, nutmeg, and sugar.

All About Takeout

From Pam

Whenever you eat in a restaurant you love, make it a policy to get to know the manager and/or the chef. One of those two people will hold the key to some of the most successful home cooking you will ever do! Not because the chef will teach you his secrets; he'll never do that, but he WILL sell them to you. Just think, you can buy, ready-to-cook in your own kitchen, anything he has chopped, stirred (for nine hours), sieved, strained, clarified, or puréed! All you have to do is take it home and take all the credit.

We have always availed ourselves of the services our local restaurants provide. But until we were faced with writing *The Phony Gourmet,* we were afraid to ask for some of the uncooked food at fancy restaurants. I love the food at the London Bar and Grill in the Westin Benson Hotel in Portland, Oregon. For some reason I was scared to call and ask to talk to the head chef. Every time I got up enough nerve, I'd have to go to the bathroom or I'd think of somebody else I should call. I guess the London Bar and Grill was too intimidating to me. I'd already found out I could buy unbaked bread, pastry and whole pies at my favorite bakery. I had learned I could buy barbecue sauce from Tony Roma's, pasta and salad dressing at The Olive Garden, and virtually anything on the menu in any restaurant I've ever been in ... but the London Bar and Grill was such a step above. Finally, I swallowed my pride and made the call.

Ring, ring, ring.
"Westin Benson."
"May I speak with the head chef?"
"One moment, please."
I waited, wondering if I would be able to understand the person who would come on the line.
"Kitchen."
"Hello, may I please speak with the head chef, if it's not too much trouble and it's an appropriate time, because I wouldn't want to be calling when he, or she, if it's a wo—"
"This is Xavier."
"Hi, my name is Pam Young and I'm writing a cookbook with my sister, Peggy Jones, called The Phony Gourmet.*"*
"Hmmmm?"
"I love your cooking and I was just wondering if you would ever consider selling your food uncooked and ready to pop into my oven at home?"

"It eez very unusual request. I never hear before."
"Well, you may be hearing it more often once this book comes out. So, would you let me take something you have prepared but haven't cooked yet?"
"Sure, but you would have to give me ample notice."
"Like how much? Two weeks?"
"Oh, no, twenty-four hours would be good."

That's all I needed to hear! After that call, I got brave. I called chefs up and down the East and West Coasts and I found out that my request was unusual but absolutely possible as long as there was a twenty-four-hour warning. Out of the fifteen calls I made, I ran into just one chef-troll. She was the head chef in a four-star restaurant in a city that shall remain nameless.

Once you feel comfortable working with your favorite chefs, you will have ascended to a whole new level of cooking in your own kitchen. Your family and friends will be thrilled to be dining on the best food money can buy, without having to get all dressed up. Oh, and if a guest wants a recipe, just give them a map to the restaurant.

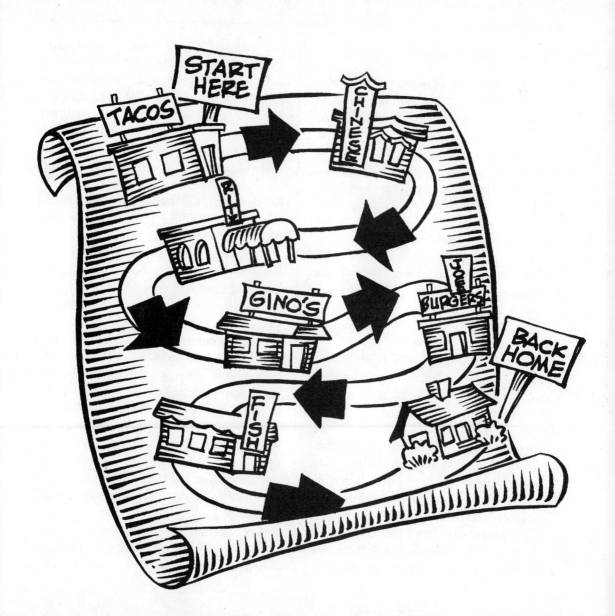

All About Stir-Frying

Stir-frying is the Chinese technique of continuous stirring, turning, and light tossing of foods one at a time in hot oil in a wok. When one food is heated through, it is pushed up the sloping sides, where it will remain warm while the other foods are stir-fried. When each food has been stir-fried, all are recombined, a sauce is added, and the dish is served at once. "Never allow anyone to cause you to doubt your ability to wok." . . . Wok Man Du.

Mastering the technique of stir-frying food sizzles down to three things: 1. keep it small, 2. keep it in order, and 3. keep it moving.

1. Cutting the food to the right size is important to the Chinese because they don't use knives and forks at the table. When they sit down to a pile of food, they're at the mercy of the guy in the kitchen, because whatever they can pinch with their chopsticks and hang on to, has to fit in their mouth and be chewed. Based on that, everything must be precut into bite-size pieces before it ever hits a hot wok.

The Chinese also know that the smaller they cut stuff, the more surfaces there will be. Even though we're Caucasian, we know that you can't throw a slab of meat into a hot pan, sear it, and expect it to be anything but tough and tasteless. We're not surprised that we have never had to muscle a piece of meat in a Chinese restaurant. From our experience, the only times we've been in restaurants where we've had to put wads of partially chewed meat in our napkins were those times when neon signs had lured us off the freeway by fluorescing things like DIESEL, DUMPING, & THE BIGGEST T-BONES IN TOWN!

Following the Chinese lead, we have learned that big isn't better and that all pieces of meat and vegetables used in one stir-fried recipe should be cut into similar shapes and sizes. If a vegetable is cubed, the meat is cut into cubes too. If vegetables are cut into thin slices, so is the meat. The bottom line: When preparing the food for the wok, think small.

2. The key to preparing stir-fried dishes is in knowing the order in which foods are seasoned and added to the pan. Pork and beef are usually marinated for 20 to 30 minutes while the vegetables are being cut. (Chicken and shrimp usually are not marinated.)

The first thing to put in the wok is the oil, swirling it up the sides of the pan. When the oil is hot, fresh ginger and a clove of garlic may then be added and browned to give the oil flavor. Take them out before you start cooking because there's nothing worse than chomping down on a hunk of gingerroot or the mush of a cooked piece of garlic while you're trying to enjoy a crispy stir-fry dish. If ginger and garlic have flavored the oil, don't put

them in the marinade or use them as an ingredient. Just like Liberace's sequins, too much of a good thing is hard to take. Stir-fry the fresh vegetables in order of fleshiness: First to crash into the hot oil in the wok are sturdy vegetables like white button mushrooms, celery, carrots, asparagus, broccoli, water chestnuts, and the like; then the more sissy vegetables such as scallions and snow peas and peppers can dive in at the last minute. Each vegetable cooks for only a minute or two and then is pushed up the sides of the wok to keep warm.

Chicken, beef, and shrimp are always stir-fried last, but pork is always stir-fried before the vegetables, then pushed up the sides to be sure it is well cooked. Chicken and beef stir-fry for only 3 to 4 minutes, shrimp only 1 or 2.

When the meat is done, all the vegetables (which have remained crisp) are mixed together with the meat in the wok. A sauce made of stock, cornstarch in cold water, and possibly some seasonings or wine is stirred together and added all at once. Everything is heated just until the sauce boils and becomes transparent and thickened.

3. Never turn your back on a wok! Stir-frying requires your complete attention.

The food will cook quickly, but it must be constantly stirred, turned, and lightly tossed.

All About the Power of Food Coloring

Our book wouldn't be complete without telling you about the power food coloring can have in your life. Did you know margarine is really white? What would your family think if you put a cube of white margarine on the table? When we were very young our mother could not buy margarine that was yellow. She had to break a red caplet of food dye into a plastic bag of white margarine and sometimes we'd get to squeeze around the color until the stuff in the bag turned the color of butter.

You can use the little bottles of liquid pigment for far more creative purposes than to make margarine look like butter. For instance, when boiling pasta, you can add a few drops of yellow food coloring to the pot and it will give the pasta a rich buttery color. With the right drops, you'll be able to instill laughter and joy among family members at especially festive times. You'll have the opportunity to teach valuable life lessons such as the one that can be learned by serving Spooky Tortilla Pie (see Index). If you have trouble communicating some of the subtler issues between husband and wife, you will be able to break the communications barrier and get your spouse's attention after reading the psychological uses of food coloring.

FESTIVE USES OF FOOD COLORING

When using food coloring for fun, don't worry that some of the foods you serve will incite some confused looks from your family. On St. Patrick's Day many years ago we both decided to serve all green food, and both of our families wondered if we'd been into the catnip. The best way to prepare an all green meal is by using white food and dyeing it green with green food coloring. White rice, pasta, cottage cheese, filet of sole, halibut, pork, mashed potatoes, and other foods will all cooperate nicely with your green dye job. Some foods, of course, are already green, like peas, broccoli, green beans, and many other vegetables. To dye butter or margarine green, use a few drops of blue food coloring (yellow and blue make green). Lime Jell-O is a nice addition to this festival of green, and don't forget to dye the children's milk and everyone's water green. Serve pistachio ice cream or grasshopper pie for dessert. Until you've seen an all green meal sitting in front of everyone at the table, you can't know the fun you're missing.

THE FOURTH OF JULY

Think red, white, and blue, then have a ball creating a blue pasta salad, a big bowl of fresh, sliced strawberries, white potato salad and a Jell-O salad using raspberry and blueberry Jell-O prepared according to package directions, chilled, cut into squares and topped with snowy white whipped cream.

Pasta dyes nicely after it's cooked. Use blue food coloring to dye penne (the little tubes), bows, shells, or wagon wheels. If you make a pasta salad, dye the mayonnaise blue before adding it to the pasta. If you put hard-boiled eggs into the salad, leave the yolks out or they'll turn green. Onion will take on the blue dye and so will water chestnuts, fake crab, and apple.

EASTER

Make a colorful pastel pasta salad by dyeing four separate portions of cooked pasta red, yellow, blue, and green. Have some fun with the colors and think up your own creative uses of them.

PSYCHOLOGICAL USES OF FOOD COLORING

Our experience with men has been very educational. For one thing, we have learned that the saying: "The way to a man's heart is through his stomach," is really true, but there's more. "The way to get a man to understand how you feel is to serve him food that relays that message."

Ring, ring, ring.
"Hello?"
"Sissy, guess what?"
"What?"
"Remember when we were talking on the phone last night about PMS?"
"Yeah?"
"Danny heard me say PMS, and when I got off the phone, he said, 'What airline?' Can you believe it? He thought PMS was an airline!"
"Schwoo! I guess that makes you a frequent flyer!"
"Yeah, real funny. I wish there was a way to let him know what it feels like."

Men relate to visual pictures much better than they do to a familiar female voice trying to explain complicated feelings. This is where the food coloring comes into play. Prepare a dinner of easily dyeable

food, similar to the St. Patrick's Day meal, only make each portion of food as mucky and muddy-looking as possible. By using all four colors in the food coloring package at once, you can achieve a very nice yucky mud color. The food will taste perfect, it will just look like pond sludge. It's important that at the time of serving, you say something like this: "See this plate of food? It looks like how I feel!" You will be amazed at how a picture (in a man's eyes), especially if it's food, is worth a thousand words.

All About Everything You'll Ever Need to Know

- Unless you love heavy and soggy mashed potatoes, use hot milk when mashing.
- If you want to make a flower arrangement and you aren't a florist, cut a large baking potato in half for a great holder for flower stems. Pierce the potato in several places with an ice pick. Place the potato flat side down in a vase of water. Poke stems in holes.
- Plain yogurt with fresh mint makes a delicious topping for baked potatoes.
- For homemade French fries almost as good as McDonald's, let cut potatoes soak in cold water for 30 minutes. Dry thoroughly before deep-frying. The trick that makes them crisp is frying them twice. The first time fry for 3 minutes, then blot off the grease and cool. The second time fry until golden brown.
- Having most of your foods prepared in advance is a wonderful way to entertain, but have something for your guests to smell when they arrive. See Index under room deodorizers.
- Keep a reclosable freezer bag in your freezer and add all leftover vegetables. When you have collected enough to make getting the food processor out worth your time, blend and return contents to freezer bag. Good for adding more flavor to soups and the like.
- Salt and pepper should be added at the end of any long cooking process.
- When puréeing a soup, remove the soup from the stove and allow it to cool slightly before puréeing. Any herbs or spices should be added to the soup while it is cooking and removed just before puréeing to assure fresh flavor and uniform consistency. Reheat. Stir in a chunk of butter just before serving to add a glossy finish to a hot puréed soup.
- Add 2 or 3 eggshells to soup stock and simmer for 10 minutes. The shells will help clarify the broth.
- Winter squash shells make very pretty and interesting soup tureens or salad bowls.
- Aluminum foil placed under the napkin in a bread basket will keep rolls warm longer.
- Mash overripe bananas, add a little lemon juice, and freeze in a reclosable freezer bag for use in cake or bread recipes.
- Warm a knife when cutting cheese, and you will find that the cheese cuts as easily as butter.

- To prevent mold, store cheese in reclosable freezer bags with some sugar cubes.
- Brush a little oil on the grater or the blade in the food processor before grating, and the cheese will wash off easily.
- Egg whites will have more volume if they are at room temperature before beating.
- To hard-boil eggs without having them form gray around the yolk, put the eggs in a small saucepan and cover with water. Bring to a boil. Cover the pan, turn off the heat, and let the eggs stand 15 to 20 minutes. Immediately plunge them into cold water.
- When hard-boiling eggs for deviled eggs, stir the eggs around while the water is boiling to keep the yolks centered.
- Place salad dressing in the bottom of the bowl with layers of ingredients on top. Toss just before serving.
- Grate citrus rinds and freeze for use when needed.
- To prevent strong odors while cooking broccoli or cabbage, place a small cup of vinegar on the range (not on a burner) or add a wedge of lemon or a stalk of celery to the pot.
- Snip chives with scissors; chopping crushes out the juice.
- To remove corn silk, dampen a toothbrush and brush downward on the cob of corn. Every strand should come off.
- To maintain their color when cooking artichokes or red vegetables, add a tablespoon of vinegar to the cooking water.
- For prime mushrooms, buy only those with closed caps. The gills should not be showing.
- Use leftover mashed potatoes by making patties and coating with flour. Freeze for frying potato cakes later.
- Chilled onions cause fewer tears when cutting.
- To add a delicious combination of flavors to cooked vegetables, mix 1 teaspoon of fresh chopped dill, 2 teaspoons of fresh lemon juice, and 1 teaspoon of Dijon-style mustard with a cube of butter that has been softened. Add to cooked vegetables before serving, and toss.
- Squeeze fresh lemon juice over steamed vegetables and toss with butter for a special touch.
- To keep cauliflower snow-white, add a little milk during boiling.
- When serving artichokes, use the arti-

choke as the bowl. Just remove the choke after cooking and spoon your favorite filling into the cavity.

- If fresh vegetables are wilted or blemished, pick off the brown edges and soak the vegetables for an hour in cold water, the juice of a lemon, or a few tablespoons of vinegar.
- For pasta cooking, the water should be boiling furiously before you add 1½ tablespoons salt and 1 tablespoon oil. After adding the pasta, maintain a steady boil and cook uncovered, stirring occasionally with wooden spoon or fork.
- As with other dried foods, the yield of the finished product is greater than fresh. One pound of dry pasta will yield about 2.2 pounds of cooked pasta.
- One pound of pasta will serve 4 people as a main course.
- A pound of pasta must be cooked in a deep pot containing 5 to 6 quarts of water. One tablespoon of butter or oil in the water will keep the noodles from boiling over.
- To hold cooked pasta, toss it with butter after draining, return it to the pot, and cover. Keep the pasta in a 175-degree oven no more than 30 minutes.
- Cooked pasta will keep for a week to 10 days if securely wrapped and refrigerated. It will keep for 6 months if frozen.
- When preparing noodles for a casserole, reduce the cooking time by a third. They will finish cooking in the oven.
- Drain but do not rinse pasta, except for salad use.
- For a special rice, add 2 tablespoons of white wine or sherry to the uncooked rice and butter in the pan. Add liquid and cook as usual.
- Freshly grated Parmesan cheese can also be purchased in the deli section of large grocery stores.
- To hull strawberries, pull up on the green stem. If the berry is ripe, the white, pulpy core will come out too. If berries are less ripe, the stems may be cut off, leaving the core inside.
- Maximum freezer storage for poultry is 6 to 8 months.
- For roasting, use a shallow pan. It allows heat to circulate around the roast.
- As a special sauce for browned meats, add ¼ cup dry white or red wine to the pan. Whisk in a tablespoon of butter, a few herbs, and ¼ cup of cream.
- Instead of using a metal rack in a roasting pan, make a grid of carrot and cel-

ery sticks and place meat or poultry on the vegetables. The additional advantage is that the vegetables flavor the pan drippings.

- Wine adds delicious flavor to almost all foods. As it cooks, the alcohol evaporates, leaving a mellow taste.
- Send cookies by mail in popcorn to keep them from breaking.
- A leek looks like a huge green onion. Use leeks in soups and stews for the mildly pungent succulent flavor in their leaves and cylindrical stalks. Cut the ends off and cut the leeks in half lengthwise, removing the very center part, as it is rather bitter. Wash thoroughly in running water. Slice thinly.
- If chocolate should stiffen while it is melting, salvage it by adding 1 teaspoon of shortening, such as Crisco, for each ounce of chocolate.
- A purple cabbage makes a colorful bowl for dip or coleslaw. Just pull back several layers of the outside leaves and remove the cabbage heart. Purple cabbage also makes a colorful and delicious coleslaw.
- Any time a recipe tells you to "fold in," it's a red flag that you're supposed to be careful with the stuff in the bowl. The goal is to incorporate a delicate substance such as whipped cream or whipped egg whites into another substance without releasing the air bubbles you've just beaten in, which would cause the whole thing to go flat. Using a rubber spatula, GENTLY bring part of the mixture from the bottom of the bowl to the top. Repeat the motion while slowly turning the bowl, until the ingredients are thoroughly blended. If you can't be gentle, pick a different recipe.

All About Nutrition

PAM AND PEGGY'S GLOSSARY OF NUTRITION

Ascorbic acid—what you get all over yourself when you open an old flashlight

Caffeine—the most popular counselor at Girl Scout camp

Calcium—dishwasher detergent

Calorie—if you don't know what that is, you're probably fat

Carbohydrate—something that falls off of a truck and can be found alongside the freeway

Glucose—interior latex enamel

Milligram—a pleasant way to keep in touch

Minerals—the black stuff that gets caught in the little round faucet screen

Monosodium glutamate—an illness that Candy Collins and Hermie Flager spread through Fort Vancouver High in the spring of 1961

Polyunsaturates—waterproof leisure suits from the seventies

Preservative—something that makes food last longer than you will if you eat it

APPETIZERS CAN SAVE
A MARRIAGE

We think that appetizers can save troubled marriages and more! Every day, in cities and towns across America, police forces spend great amounts of time and energy responding to family disturbance calls. We think that appetizers could substantially reduce their work in that area. In fact, we don't think *Cops* (the TV show) would be able to stay on the air if more people started serving hors d'oeuvres more often.

An appetizer can be as simple as part of dinner cut on the bias or stuck on a skewer and served with something to drink. For your family, an hors d'oeuvre can take the when-will-dinner-be-ready edge off hungry people. For company, appetizers should be served with a little flair (parsley will do).

La Viande D'hier Soir Est Sous le Fromage

(The Meat from Last Night Is Under the Cheese)

One of the best things to do with left-overs is to hide them under your favorite cheese, brown, and serve the next night as an hors d'oeuvre.

PREPARATION TIME: 5 minutes
COOKING TIME: 5 minutes
SERVES: Depends on how much viande was left over

Triscuits
Leftover meat, cut into bite-size pieces
Cheese of your choice, sliced thinly and just a little smaller than a Triscuit

1. Preheat the broiler. Place the Triscuits on an ungreased cookie sheet. Place the meat on the crackers and top with the cheese.
2. Place a rack as high as possible in the oven. Broil until cheese melts and starts to turn brown.

Tip: Leave the oven door open and watch the appetizers closely because they turn brown quickly.

Clams Pocahontas

From Peggy

Ring, ring, ring.

"Hello?"
"Sissy, are you doing Clams Pocahontas or am I?"
"I don't care. Do you want to?"
"Well, I just finished writing about Oysters Rockefeller and since I'm into shell-fish, I can go ahead and do the clams."
"Great. I'll work on Spooky Tortilla Pie."

I hung up from my coauthor and sister and pulled the recipe for Clams Pocahontas from the seafood corner of my brain. The formula has been in our family for as long as I can remember.

Of course, there's nothing better than cooking these steamers on an open camp-fire, but for now, enjoy the taste you'll get from your indoor stove.

PREPARATION TIME: 5 minutes
COOKING TIME: 5 minutes
SERVES: 4 to 6

4 *pounds small steamer clams*
2 *tablespoons butter*
2 *cups beef stock*
1 *teaspoon Lawry's Garlic Powder Coarse*
    Ground with Parsley
¼ *teaspoon cayenne pepper*
2 *chorizo sausages, cooked and crumbled*

1. Wash the clams in cold water.
2. In an 8-quart kettle, bring the butter, beef stock, garlic, pepper, and sausages to a boil over high heat. Add the clams, cover, and cook until the shells open, about 5 minutes.

Serve in individual bowls, making sure each person gets some of the broth. Let diners tear off pieces of a large loaf of French bread and dunk it in the broth.

Fighting Dragon Pot Stickers
From Peggy

This recipe for pot stickers is one you can't EXACTLY duplicate unless you live in Hazel Dell, Washington, or you're within driving distance of the Fighting Dragon restaurant there. It's really called the Golden Crane, but one time Danny and I had a big fight in the parking lot over something stupid and we never got out of the car. We went home mad and hungry, and from then on the name was changed.

If you love Chinese food, you have probably found your own favorite restaurant and the people there know you. Ask them if you can buy their pot stickers, egg rolls, wontons, or anything else you could impress company with, and get them to tell you how they're prepared. At our restaurant, Dominic (the owner) even took me back into the kitchen and let me watch him cook. Then he sold me the frozen stickers and the dipping sauce for 50 cents less per order than they cost on the menu.

I'd only do this recipe as a company showoff presentation, because I don't want to make these delicacies too mundane. If we could eat them at home anytime we wanted, why would we go out? I don't want to spoil a good thing because eating out is one of my favorite things to do. Even though Danny isn't as anxious as I am to leave the home trough and let somebody else do the cooking, he can still come home from a long day at work and if I say, "How about some pot stickers at the Fighting Dragon?" he rallies.

When you serve the most delicious pot stickers in town, you'll gain the reputation of a gourmet cook with an international flair.

PREPARATION TIME: depends on how close you are to your favorite Chinese restaurant
COOKING TIME: 15 minutes
SERVES: 4 as an appetizer

2   teaspoons vegetable oil
16 frozen pot stickers
2   cups chicken broth
Sauce from restaurant

1. In a large skillet or wok, heat the vegetable oil over high heat, swirling it around to coat the pan. When it's hot, add the frozen pot stickers and stir-fry for about 30 seconds.
2. Cover pot stickers with chicken broth. Put a lid on the pan and simmer on low heat for 10 minutes.
3. Pour off the broth except for about 2 tablespoons. In the same skillet, pan-fry the cooked pot stickers on low heat until golden brown.

Serve with the sauce from the restaurant for dipping.

Le Pâté

Delicate texture with a burst of flavor. Guests will go gaga over this one, but the secret ingredient can NEVER be told!

PREPARATION TIME: 4 minutes
SERVES: 4

2   (2¹/₂-ounce) jars Gerber Beef Baby
      Food (2nd foods variety)
1¹/₂ teaspoons Lawry's Garlic
      Powder Coarse Ground with
      Parsley
¹/₄ teaspoon cayenne pepper
¹/₄ teaspoon Lawry's Seasoned
      Salt
2   tablespoons Best Foods or
      Hellmann's Mayonnaise
1   tablespoon fresh lemon juice

In a small bowl, mix all ingredients thoroughly. Serve with appetizer crackers and PROMISE never to tell.

Mushrooms with a Heart

From Pam

If you don't like giblets, forget this one, but if you are a chicken heart lover and you KNOW that EVERYONE would love them (even those who say they wouldn't, but would if they didn't know what they really were), you must try this "sleight of heart" taste trick.

First, let's address the squeamish eater. Out of our six kids, there was only one real squeamer, Joanna. The list of foods that could bring on her gagging reflex was endless. The best way to get the gaggers into her, with their valuable vitamins and nutrients, was to buy a food processor and purée the identity out of them. Most children are not as bad as Joanna was and we're pleased to report that as an adult, she has made friends with many of her childhood food enemies.

As adults, most of us have a fairly toler-

ant palate, but there is a line that is drawn somewhere right around giblets. That's probably why we call them giblets and not vital chicken organs, and why we call squid calamari, and calves veal.

We think the reason American restaurants list snails on the appetizer fare as "ESCARGOT" is because they know that if their menus read "SNAILS," they'd have zero takers. While this goes on in the States, the reverse is probably happening in France. "SNAILS" or even "SLUGS WITH A SHELL" are probably touted in the poshest, candlelit establishments, luring French-born, non-English-speaking diners into orders that would never happen if the menus read "ESCARGOT."

On a personal note, we have learned in feeding the squeamish that they'll eat and enjoy many foods as long as they don't know what they're eating. We have to admit that our basic recipe for the chicken hearts was not very popular, even with the most daredevilish eaters, because a plate of chicken hearts, no matter how delicious, looks more like a serving of marinated rabbit droppings. While wrapping up the yummy leftover coronary organs after several parties, we thought up the idea of hiding the delicious little delicacies in a tasty mushroom camouflage. After taking a tray of these extraordinary appetizers to a party or serving them in your own home, you'll be bombarded with praise— unless of course your guests don't like mushrooms!

Served hot, they're fabulous. Served cold, they're even better.

PREPARATION TIME: 15 minutes
COOKING TIME: 30 minutes
SERVES: It depends on who gets to them first

36 mushrooms
1 package Schilling Meat Marinade
1 tablespoon olive oil
1 tablespoon vinegar
1/2 cup white wine
1/2 cup chopped onion
36 chicken hearts (3/4 pound to 1 pound)

TOPPING:
1/2 teaspoon Lawry's Seasoned Salt
1 teaspoon Lawry's Garlic Powder Coarse Ground with Parsley
1/4 teaspoon pepper
1 tablespoon Worcestershire sauce
6 ounces Philadelphia Brand Cream Cheese, softened
1 cup bread crumbs

1. Wash the mushrooms and pop out the stems. Set both aside.
2. In a large skillet, heat the package of meat marinade, the oil, vinegar, white wine, and onions over medium heat, mixing thoroughly. Add the chicken hearts, mushrooms, and stems. Cover and simmer 10 minutes.
3. Remove the mushrooms and stems with a slotted spoon. Continue cooking the chicken hearts for another 20 minutes, or until tender. Remove chicken hearts with the slotted spoon. Cool.
4. In a food processor, prepare topping: Blend everything left in the frying pan with seasoned salt, garlic, pepper, Worcestershire Sauce, cream cheese, and bread crumbs.
5. Stuff the hearts in each mushroom cavity with the blend in the frying pan. Hide each heart with the remaining cream cheese topping and push a stem into the topping. Just before serving, place under the broiler until the topping bubbles and browns slightly.

WORK ALERT: In Step 4, process the mushroom stems in with the other ingredients, eliminating pushing the stems into topping. The mushrooms look very cute with stems in them, but sometimes time is more important than cuteness.

Leeky Dip with Clams

Don't let the name scare you. This leek and clam dip is scrumptious!

PREPARATION TIME: 2 minutes
CHILLING TIME: 2 hours
MAKES: 2½ cups

1 package Knorr Leek Soup
2 cups sour cream
1 (6½-ounce) can minced clams, drained

In a small bowl, mix soup, sour cream, and clams. Stir until blended. Cover; chill 2 hours. Stir before serving.

Carol Story's Hors D'oeuvres

Carol Story, our good friend and a producer of *CBS Morning News,* wanted us to show how to make creative hors d'oeuvres for a Christmas party. We came up with five ideas that were so popular with viewers that we are still getting calls on the recipes, and it's a year later!

A snowman made of dip is the edible centerpiece of this edible hors d'oeuvre table presentation. The pepperoni log cabin stands, quaint and delicious, in a yard bordered by a split-rail beef jerky fence. Santa's sleigh is really a halved acorn squash filled with colorful vegetable presents. Two additional recipes, Snowman Quiche and Log Cabin Pizza, use up any leftovers from the party for breakfast the morning after.

Cream Cheese and Garlic Snowman

Standing more that a foot tall, this delicious snowman is great to serve with raw vegetables or cocktail crackers. Guests just dip right into the snowman's body. If you're going to have a big party, make two snowpersons, Mr. and Mrs.

PREPARATION TIME: 15 minutes
SERVES: 15 party animals

2 (8-ounce) packages Philadelphia Brand
   Cream Cheese, softened
2 teaspoons Lawry's Garlic Powder Coarse
   Ground with Parsley
1 teaspoon Lawry's Seasoned Salt
1 teaspoon onion powder
⅓ cup milk
1 (8-inch round) loaf French bread
1 (5-inch round) loaf French bread
1 round French roll
¼ cup instant mashed potato flakes
1 leaf red cabbage (snowman's scarf)
1 carrot (nose)
8 peppercorns (eyes and mouth)
5 coffee beans (buttons)
2 small twigs (arms)
1 cardboard toilet paper tube (hat)
1 square of black felt (hat)
1 (15-inch) wooden skewer (spinal
   column)

1. In a medium bowl, mix together cream cheese, garlic, seasoned salt, onion powder, and milk until smooth.

2. Place the larger loaf of bread on a large serving platter. Frost with half the cream cheese mixture. Stick a wooden skewer through the middle of the large loaf. Stick the medium-size loaf onto the skewer to make the second "snowball." Frost the second ball, leaving enough cream cheese mixture to frost the third ball. Stick the French roll onto the skewer for the snowman's head. Frost, and decorate, using items as listed in the ingredients.

3. After the snowman is decorated, shake the instant potato flakes all over him. They look just like snow and are remarkably tasty with the cream cheese "frosting."

Snowman Quiche

PREPARATION TIME: 5 minutes
COOKING TIME: 30 minutes
SERVES: 6

1 Snowman's remains, refrigerated after the
   party
6 eggs, beaten
1 cup milk

1. Butter a medium-size baking dish. Tear up the snowman into bite-size pieces and place in the dish. (The pieces will have leftover dip on them, which will add a tantalizing flavor to this dish.)

2. Mix milk and eggs together. Pour the mixture over the dismembered snowman. Bake in a 400-degree oven for 25 minutes.

Acorn Squash Sleigh

1. Cut the acorn squash in half lengthwise. Scoop out the seeds, slime, and pulp, leaving a ½-inch-thick shell on one of the halves.
2. Cut the other half into 2 sections, following the natural grooves in the squash. These make great sleigh runners. Attach each "runner" to the hollowed-out half with toothpicks.
3. Fill the sleigh with carrot sticks and celery sticks.

1. Cut acorn squash in half. Cut one half into segments to form runners.

2. Fill with broccoli, carrot sticks, and cherry tomatoes.

3. Use toothpicks as supports for runners.

Pepperoni A-Frame Log Cabin

Instead of a traditional gingerbread house, make this easy A-frame log cabin out of pepperoni, crackers, and cheese.

PREPARATION TIME: 1 hour
SERVES: 25

⅓ of a 5-pound brick Tillamook Cheddar Cheese (see Note)
2 (8-ounce) packages Philadelphia Brand Cream Cheese
Approximately 4 board feet of pepperoni (48 inches)
1 (12-ounce) package Ritz Crackers
1 Chicken in a Biskit cracker (the door)
2 Cheez-It crackers (the windows)
¾ cup instant potato flakes (snow in the yard)
12 6-inch pieces of beef jerky

Cabin Foundation
Cut a 4-inch piece of cheese for the foundation of the cabin. The brick of cheese is already 4 inches wide, so you will end up with a 4-inch square block.

Log Siding

1. Cut the pepperoni sticks into ten 5-inch-long pieces and four 4½-inch-long pieces. Using cream cheese as mortar, smear a generous amount on two opposite sides of Cheddar cheese foundation. (The other two sides will be covered by the long A-frame roof.)

2. Press the 5-inch pepperoni logs into the cream cheese, letting the cream cheese fill in the cracks. Cut twenty ⅛-inch circles of pepperoni to give the illusion of logs coming from the sides that don't show because of the roof. Use cream cheese to stick them on (see illustration).

3. Work from the bottom and build up 5 logs on each side. Place the four remaining 4½-inch logs on last, 2 on each side. (Those logs are shorter in order to clear the roof.)

Cabin Roof

1. Cut a 4 × 19-inch rectangle out of heavy cardboard. (Two standard business envelopes, when put end to end, make a 4 × 19-inch rectangle.) Out of heavy cardboard, cut 2 triangles with a base of 4 inches and 2 equal sides of 4¾ inches. These triangles will fit into the space in the top of the A-frame on either side of the cabin. Secure the roof to the cheese foundation with toothpicks. (Use an ice pick to make holes, so the toothpicks won't break while you jam them through the cardboard into the cheese.)

2. Smear a heavy layer of cream cheese on the cardboard roof and shingle it, beginning at the bottom, using Ritz crackers.

Door and Windows

1. Stick on the Chicken in a Biskit door with cream cheese.

2. For the windows, stick both Cheez-Its on with cream cheese.

Split-Rail Beef Jerky Fence

Layer the beef jerky so that it looks like a split-rail fence.

Note: A 5-pound brick of cheese may seem like a lot of cheese, but remember it freezes well. Leave the remainder of the brick of cheese at room temperature for about 2 hours to soften. Shred, using a food processor. Freeze shredded cheese in reclosable freezer bags. You'll thank yourself over and over when a recipe calls for grated cheese and all you have to do is go to the freezer and measure out an amount.

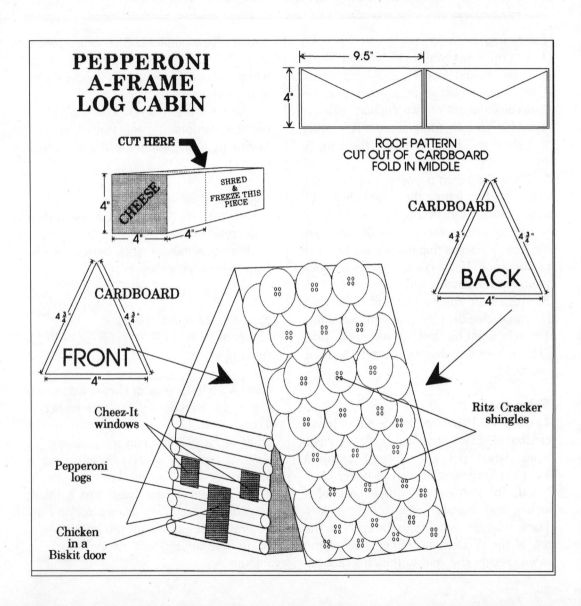

PEPPERONI A-FRAME LOG CABIN

CUT HERE

CHEESE

SHRED & FREEZE THIS PIECE

4"

4" 4"

9.5"

4"

ROOF PATTERN
CUT OUT OF CARDBOARD
FOLD IN MIDDLE

CARDBOARD

4 3/4" 4 3/4"

BACK

4"

CARDBOARD

4 3/4" 4 3/4"

FRONT

4"

Cheez-It windows

Pepperoni logs

Chicken in a Biskit door

Ritz Cracker shingles

Log Cabin Pizza

Nibble, nibble, little mouse, who made pizza out of my house?

PREPARATION TIME: 5 minutes
COOKING TIME: 18 minutes
SERVES: 4

Leftover pepperoni from log cabin
1 or 2 Totino's Party Pizzas

1. Cut up the pepperoni and distribute it evenly on pizza.
2. Follow the directions for cooking on the back of the pizza package.

Hotsy-Totsy Refried Bean Bake

Serve this one piping hot with red tortilla chips and you'll have a place in the stars with big and little dippers alike.

PREPARATION TIME: 7 minutes
COOKING TIME: 30 minutes

SERVES: 10 little dippers (5 if served as a casserole.)

1 (17-ounce) can Rosarita Refried Beans, or 2 cups South of the Border Homemade Refried Beans (see Index)
½ cup sour cream
1 (12-ounce) jar salsa (medium to hot, depending on your preference)
½ teaspoon Lawry's Garlic Powder Coarse Ground with Parsley
½ teaspoon Lawry's Seasoned Salt
½ cup finely chopped onion
1 cup grated Cheddar cheese

1. In a medium bowl, mix the beans, sour cream, salsa, garlic, seasoned salt, onion, and half the cheese. Pour into a medium-size casserole dish sprayed with Pam.
2. Bake in a 375-degree oven for 25 minutes. Top with the remaining cheese and bake 5 minutes longer, or until the cheese melts.

Cheesy Hot Clam Dip

This dip is a show-stopper! It's hot stuff and everyone will want the recipe. It's up to you whether or not you share it.

PREPARATION TIME: 5 minutes
COOKING TIME: 15 minutes
MAKES: 1½ cups

2   tablespoons olive oil
½ cup finely chopped onion
½ cup finely chopped celery
¼ pound Kraft Velveeta Cheese, cubed
2   (7½-ounce) cans clams, drained and
    minced
¼ cup Durkee Redhot Cayenne Pepper Sauce
1   tablespoon Lea & Perrins Worcestershire
    Sauce
1   tablespoon milk

1. In a medium skillet, heat the oil over medium-high heat. Add onion and celery. Sauté until tender.
2. Reduce the heat to low. Add the remaining ingredients. Continue cooking, stirring constantly, until the cheese is melted.

Tip: Serve hot with crackers.

Broccoli Dip

This wonderful dip is like nothing you or your guests have ever tasted. Unique and delicious—everyone will want the recipe!

PREPARATION TIME: 5 minutes
CHILLING TIME: 2 hours
MAKES: 4 cups

1   (10-ounce) package frozen chopped broc-
    coli, thawed and drained
1   package Knorr Leek Soup
2   cups sour cream
½ cup Best Foods or Hellmann's mayonnaise
1   (8-ounce) can water chestnuts, drained
    and chopped

In a medium mixing bowl, mix together the broccoli, soup mix, sour cream, mayonnaise, and water chestnuts. Stir until blended. Cover; chill 2 hours. Stir before serving.

Wilbur's Air Force Academy Buffalo Wings

From Peggy

Chris is a senior at the Air Force Academy. Since he's been there the word *wings* has become very important in his life. All of the cadets in the whole school make up The Wing, he got his wings because he's a cadet instructor pilot, and, finally, he's proud to have acquired a taste for Buffalo wings!

Wilbur, Chris's friend at the academy, introduced him to the spicy, hot chicken parts and for the last three years they have sampled the red devils in practically every restaurant in Colorado Springs. While Chris was home for summer leave, he was going through Buffalo wing withdrawal. To satisfy the craving, we developed our own recipe. He knew exactly what he wanted to taste. He wanted peppery, hot chicken with a kick! Since the rest of us were just getting acquainted with these fiery appendages, we insisted on moderation. While Chris would have enjoyed them even hotter, he had to agree that they were world-class Buffalo wings. In thanks to Wilbur for the introduction, we named our wings in his honor.

One portion of Wilbur's wings will trigger the craving for the rest of your life. If you dare to make them once, be prepared to make them again and again.

PREPARATION TIME: 5 minutes
MARINATING TIME: 30 minutes
GRILLING TIME: 30 minutes
SERVES: 2 cadets or 6 civilians

5 pounds chicken wings
1/2 cup butter
1 teaspoon Lawry's Garlic Powder Coarse Ground with Parsley
1 (12-ounce) bottle Durkee Redhot Cayenne Pepper Sauce
2 teaspoons Cajun's Choice Creole Seasoning

1. Remove and discard the tip portion of each chicken wing. Cut the part remaining at the joint. Rinse and pat dry with paper towels. Place the wings in a heavy-duty reclosable freezer bag.

2. In a small microwave-safe container, melt the butter. Add the garlic powder and mix.

3. Pour the bottle of pepper sauce into the freezer bag. Add the butter mixture. Seal the bag. Shake contents gently to mix. Marinate for 30 minutes, turning the bag over about every 10 minutes to distribute the marinade.

4. Using a sheet of heavy aluminum foil that has been sprayed with Pam, form a boat that will hold the sauce and wings as they cook. Place the foil boat on top of the barbecue grill. Empty the entire freezer bag into the boat. Sprinkle half the Cajun seasoning on the wings. Grill for 10 minutes, then poke several holes in the foil with a fork to allow the sauce to escape slowly onto the coals.

5. Grill another 10 minutes, turning the wings often. Sprinkle with the remaining Cajun seasoning and continue grilling 10 more minutes, still turning often. Wings are ready when they pull away easily from the bone.

Tip: If you want your wings hotter, get a torch.

SOUPS AND SALADS

Caesar's Choice

From Peggy

Danny and I used to order Caesar salads in good restaurants all the time. For years we watched the cocky captains of four-star notoriety toss their presentations tableside. Then we realized that every one we ordered was a little different.

It seemed as if these Caesar wannabes were taking license with the recipe. We also noticed that we had developed a discriminating palate for the pile of greens set before us. We found that we loved the salty jolt of an anchovy bite and the wonderful garlic flavor, married with zesty lemon and fresh ground black pepper.

We not only developed a taste for Caesar salad, but we could even tell by sight and smell if it was worthy of our recommendation. A good Caesar stands high on the plate, still crisp because it's dressed at the last minute. We found ourselves scrutinizing the tableside preparation as if Julius was our dead relative and we wanted to protect our family reputation.

Usually we'd have to request extra Parmesan, ground pepper, and croutons,

and instruct the salad magician not to hold back on the garlic and anchovies. We were used to having our requests taken in stride by the tuxedoed waiter, until we encountered Jobert (he called himself Yobear but his name tag said "Captain Jobert").

Jobert was the head waiter/salad tosser in a fancy hotel's restaurant across the street from Central Park. He liked himself almost more than he liked his position, or even his hair. We said we'd begin with a Caesar salad. He said we'd made an excellent choice. We felt proud.

When he rolled out the salad cart, which had already been prepared for him by some minimum-wager back in the kitchen, it

was covered with the various ingredients, mysteriously concealed by individual silver-domed lids. As if he were getting ready to serve communion, he prepared the salad bowl by rubbing it with garlic cloves. The dark wood looked as rich as the paneling in the movie *Arthur.*

He unveiled the romaine, which had been shrouded in cheesecloth like a lady-in-waiting. Two lemon halves, dressed in cheesecloth hats, looked as if they were on their way to an Easter parade. One by one, the silver domes were removed and the contents underneath were ceremoniously exposed.

In a magnificent flurry, Jobert tossed the proud assemblage of edibles and presented each of us with a plateful. "Enjoy," he instructed as he whirled and started to leave.

"Excuse me, Jobert, could I please have a little more ground pepper?" Danny asked.

That's when the lettuce hit the fan! It was as if Danny had said, "Yo! Bear. Get back here and gimme some more pepper!" Our indignant server informed us that he had been making Caesars for eighteen years without a complaint. Even Jackie Onassis had never altered his presentation. (Maybe she didn't like a lot of pepper.)

In our opinion, since Caesar salad was originally concocted in a frenzy by a monk who probably forgot to get groceries, it's perfectly fine to adjust the ingredients according to your own tastes—but please don't leave out the anchovies.

Caesar's Choice

We would challenge any New York Caesarean to a salad-tossing contest with our own twelve-star recipe (gleaned from watching three four-star restaurant tossers).

PREPARATION TIME: 10 minutes
SERVES: 4

2 *medium-size heads romaine lettuce*
1 *clove garlic, cut in half*
1 *tablespoon extra-virgin olive oil*
2 *egg yolks, coddled*

1 *(2-ounce) can flat fillet anchovies, drained*
2 *cloves garlic, pressed*
1 *tablespoon Lea & Perrins Worcestershire Sauce*
2 *teaspoons Dijon-style mustard*
1 *lemon, squeezed and strained*
2 *teaspoons garlic wine vinegar*
1 *teaspoon fresh ground pepper*
1 *cup The Incredible Crouton (see Index)*
1/4 *cup grated Parmesan cheese*

1. Wash romaine, pat dry with paper towels, and tear into bite-size pieces.
2. Place the lettuce in a large wooden salad bowl that has been rubbed on all surfaces with the garlic halves. Sprinkle with oil.
3. Put the raw eggs in their shells in a small bowl. Cover them with boiling water. Set aside.
4. In another small bowl, mash the anchovies between the prongs of two forks until they are the size of bacon bits at a salad bar.
5. Carefully remove the eggs from the water with a slotted spoon and separate yolks from whites, discarding the whites. Add the yolks to the anchovies. Mix.
6. To the egg-anchovy mixture, add the pressed garlic, Worcestershire sauce, mustard, lemon juice, and vinegar. Mix well.

Pour over the dry lettuce. Toss lightly to mix. Sprinkle with pepper, croutons, and cheese. Toss again.

Tip: Some things you can't cheat on in this recipe. The lemon, garlic, and Parmesan have to be fresh and the croutons have to be incredible. If you don't have time to go the second mile, wait to make this recipe until you do.

Scrumptious and Simply Simple Spinach Salad

If you serve this to children, just call it dark green-leaf salad. If they know it's spinach, they'll balk. Spinach is notorious among youngsters as something they HAVE to eat, and, as you know, if they have ever had to eat canned spinach, it can take years to get over the experience. Fresh spinach is so delicious and nutritious, and when you put this spinach salad in front of your kids (with an alias), they will love it and ask for more.

YOU will even think you should've worked hard for the taste you get with this simple dressing.

PREPARATION TIME: 6 minutes
SERVES: 4

½ cup mayonnaise
2 tablespoons sugar
2 tablespoons white wine vinegar
½ teaspoon Lawry's Garlic Powder Coarse
*   Ground with Parsley*
1 bunch fresh spinach (about 5 cups)
1 small red onion, thinly sliced

1. In a small mixing bowl, combine the mayonnaise, sugar, vinegar, and garlic. Chill.
2. Pinch off the stems at the base of each spinach leaf. Wash the spinach leaves thoroughly. Dry on paper towels.
3. Put the onion circles and spinach leaves (torn into bite-size pieces) into a salad bowl.
4. Just before serving, pour the dressing on the spinach and toss.

Tip: Crumble ¼ cup crisp bacon over salad for a yummy touch.

Homemade Chicken Stock

To have on hand about a month's supply of white chicken meat, you'll need to buy about 20 chicken breast halves when they're cheap. Don't throw the skin and bones away! They will not only provide the flavor and nutrients for more than a month's supply of chicken stock, but they will also fill your whole house with the tranquil and comforting aroma of chicken soup.

The longer it simmers, the better it gets! Use whenever a recipe calls for chicken stock.

PREPARATION TIME: 20 minutes
COOKING TIME: 3 hours
MAKES: 5 quarts chicken stock
       3 cups cooked white meat
       6 cups dog or cat food

20 *chicken breast halves, with skin and bones*
3   *whole cloves garlic*
2   *medium onions, quartered*
4   *stalks celery, quartered*
2   *bay leaves*
1   *tablespoon Lawry's Seasoned Salt*
1   *teaspoon pepper*
5   *quarts water*

1. Skin and bone the breasts. Freeze meal-size portions of uncooked breast meat in reclosable freezer bags.

2. In a 12-quart stock pot, simmer the bones, skin, garlic cloves, onions, celery, bay leaves, seasoned salt, pepper, and water on medium-low heat for 3 hours. (It won't hurt if it goes 4.)

3. Pour the broth into a large bowl or pot, using a colander to separate the liquid from the solids. Refrigerate the stock.

4. When the stock is chilled, take the hardened fat off the top and, to make sure there is enough expansion room for freezing, fill quart-size reclosable freezer bags or quart jars with about 3 cups of stock.

5. Pick through the bones, separating gristle and skin (for dogs and cats) from white meat that didn't get cut off in the boning process. Freeze single portions of dog and cat food in reclosable freezer bags. Freeze the white meat for use in casseroles, soups, or salads. (Don't forget to label the packages or Fido will think he's won the lottery and your Chicken Cordon Bleu will be tough to chew.)

Carol Story's Manhattan Lobster Bisque

"There's not a drop of lobster in this delicious soup, but if you tell your guests it's called Lobster Bisque, their brains will take over and they will actually think that's what's in it." —CAROL STORY

PREPARATION TIME: 4 minutes
COOKING TIME: 15 minutes
SERVES: 4

1 (10-ounce) can Campbell's Tomato Soup
1 (10-ounce) can Campbell's Split Pea Soup
2 cups milk
1 cup fake crab, finely chopped in food
*   processor*

1. In a medium saucepan, heat soups, milk, and fake crab over medium heat for 15 minutes, or until steaming hot.
2. Serve piping hot and don't forget to tell everyone the name of the recipe.

Tip: Great with a few of The Incredible Crouton(s) (see Index) sprinkled on top.

Classic Chunky Chicken Soup with Tortellini

From Peggy

Chicken soup heals. I know it does. Whenever I make a great big kettle of it, everybody feels better. I subscribe to *Victoria* magazine and when I got the May issue the cover title was "Celebrating a Mother's Quiet Acts of Love" and I thought, "Yep, that's gonna be about making chicken soup." It wasn't, but I think it should have been. I make my soup from squeeze. I buy a fabulous soup base concentrate in the refrigerated section of the grocery store and squeeze it into my own stockpot. (That's the quiet part of my act. The mother's love part is added later.)

My favorite of the soup base concentrates is made by Classic Soups. Their different varieties are called Stockpot Soups. I knew they'd be good when I read the back of the package:

Stockpot Soups began as a supplier of fresh, delicious, wholesome soups to fine restaurants throughout the United

States. Our soups have been so popular that we are now selling them world-wide. Now these soups are available for you to make at home. Stockpot Soups combine farm-fresh vegetables, real dairy products, delicate seasonings and top-grade meat, poultry and seafood with time-tested recipes to create these delicious, healthy soups. We believe in freshness and taste, therefore we don't add preservatives or additives.

The ingredients listed on the package are: fresh tortellini, water, fresh carrots, fresh celery, fresh onions, natural chicken flavoring, modified food starch, green beans, margarine, granulated garlic, spices, parsley. Why would any busy mother in her right mind spend the day slumped over a stockpot when she could get the same (or better) results with one squeeze and a few of her own personal touches? For personal touches, which also disguise the commercial product, I spin off the package ingredients, and add more of the same stuff.

Keep it quiet about how you made this soup, then let the love part come through when you serve it to your family. This is a perfect example of convenience food at its best!

PREPARATION TIME: 5 minutes
COOKING TIME: 25 minutes
SERVES: 6

1   (16-ounce) package Classic Soups
      Tortellini Vegetable Stockpot Soup
      Concentrate
1   quart water
1   (10¾-ounce) can Campbell's Cream of
      Chicken Soup
1   cup milk
4   chicken breast halves, skinned, boned,
      and cut into bite-size pieces
½   cup chopped onion
1   chopped celery stalk
½   teaspoon Lawry's Garlic Powder Coarse
      Ground with Parsley

1. Into a large stockpot, squeeze the contents of the package of concentrated soup base. Add the water. Bring to a boil and hold the boil for 5 minutes.
2. Add the canned soup, milk, chicken pieces, onion, celery, and garlic powder. Simmer 20 minutes.

Good served with warm garlic bread.

WHAT'S FOR DINNER?

Savory Couch Potato Stew

From Pam

In 1976, I was married to a very demanding person who gets a great deal of credit for compelling me to create many recipes that gave the illusion that I worked much harder than I did. This is one of them.

Our children were three, eight, and eleven, and on this particular Saturday, my sister and I had planned to take our six kids on a garage sale day, an outing that was never sanctioned by Mr. Cranky. He had left for work about 7:00 A.M. and my plan was to play all day and beat him home in time

for dinner. Notice that I said "in time for," not "in time to fix" dinner. Unfortunately, it was common for me to have a plan like that, which didn't include meal preparation time.

I thought about dinner at 8:30 A.M., just as Peggy drove into the driveway to pick me up for our big day out. I pictured the Crankster coming home at 5:00 P.M., antagonistic and obsessed with the quest for food. I saw myself racing around paranoid, pathetic, and planless. But before she could uncarseat her three kids (all under three), I had the kettle in the oven. It was such a hit that I've been making it ever since.

It isn't necessary, but it is impressive to put a pastry top on this stew. From a sheet of Pepperidge Farm frozen Puff Pastry, cut a circle the size of your crockery cooker or heavy kettle. When you put a tender crust on anything, it's like signing a painting if you're a famous artist, putting on a top hat, walking an Afghan hound, wearing a push-up bra, or having illegible handwriting if you are a doctor or lawyer. It makes a definite statement. A pastry top will ALWAYS give the illusion of hard work, and it's well worth the minimal effort.

This hearty stew will greet your senses when you come home from a busy day. Its tantalizing aroma will melt away any stress you've collected and waft throughout your entire neighborhood. Be prepared for drooling drop-ins!

PREPARATION TIME: 5 minutes
COOKING TIME: 6 to 8 hours
SERVES: 6

3 pounds boneless chuck roast, trimmed of all fat
10 small new potatoes
10 baby carrots
3 stalks celery, quartered
1 large onion, quartered
1 package Lipton Onion Soup Mix
1 (10 ¾-ounce) can Campbell's Cream of Mushroom Soup

1½ teaspoons Lawry's Garlic Powder Coarse Ground with Parsley
2 beef bouillon cubes
4 to 5 cups water
1 (20-ounce) package frozen mixed vegetables
1 sheet Pepperidge Farm frozen Puff Pastry (optional)

1. Place the roast in a heavy 4- or 5-quart kettle or crockery cooker. Add the potatoes, carrots, celery, onion, onion soup mix, canned soup, garlic, bouillon cubes, and enough water to cover all ingredients. Cover and slow-cook in a 275-degree oven or on low setting in crockery cooker for 6 to 8 hours.
2. Twenty minutes before serving, add the package of frozen mixed vegetables.

Optional Pepperidge Farm Show-off Top:
Preheat oven to 400 degrees. Thaw a pastry sheet for 20 minutes on a floured board. Cut a circle to fit the top of kettle or crockery cooker (if it's a removable, ovenproof crock) and fold in half. Cut vent holes across the fold and open back up into a circle. Place directly on the stew and bake for 20 minutes.

Camelot Stew

From Pam

This stew evolved out of leftovers from an elegant dinner that included French onion soup and filet mignon. I threw the two together, added some vegetable stock with a little cornstarch to thicken it, and the result was almost mystical. The first time I served the official Camelot stew to company was when I had my former husband's former boss and his former wife over for dinner. They were absolutely whirlblasted away with the meal as they savored each bite.

I think that it's probably not a good idea to share the secret ingredient with anyone. I do regret that I ever told the woman what was in the stew, because after dinner, when the guys went off to talk about business, she turned on me.

"Oh, Pam, How—? Where—? What was in that stew that made it so delicious?"

"Well, I used meat that one wouldn't ordinarily put in a stew."

"Oh, I suppose it was elk or something?"

"No."

"Deer?"

"No."

"Bear?"

"No."

"Well, what then?"

Something told me not to tell her what it was, but I was so proud of my invention that I smiled and blabbed, "Filet mignon."

She was disgusted. "Well, no wonder it's so good! I guess if you put filet mignon in anything it would make it taste fabulous." She probably thought, "How much money is my husband paying that clown. Here I am shopping at Pelky's Food Barn and she's on a Champagne and caviar budget."

If I had it to do over, I would have told her that it was a treasured family secret.

The second time I served Camelot stew was at a Christmas caroling party I had for the neighborhood. It was a mistake to serve the stew, because I wasn't financially prepared to watch the expensive meat disappear into a pair of noncarolers I barely knew from down the road. There's nothing more exasperating than to watch two stew hogs hover over the pot and devour your filet mignon like it's chuck. Since it would be inappropriate to have a guard stand by the kettle, it's better to serve this stew to people who will take the time to appreciate the secret cut that's in it.

An extraordinarily delicious vegetarian stew, until you add filet mignon at the last minute. Then you have a meal fit to serve royal carnivores. Imagine the queen asking, "What is this INCREDIBLE flavor and where in London did you get stew meat this tender?"

PREPARATION TIME: 15 minutes
COOKING TIME: 1½ hours
SERVES: 6—one king, one queen, a couple of princes or princesses, and a lord or two. (No peasants, please!)

2 tablespoons butter
3 medium onions, thinly sliced
3 stalks celery, thinly sliced
1 (1-ounce) package Knorr Pepper Sauce Mix
5 cups water
4 Knorr Vegetarian Vegetable Bouillon Cubes
2 cups halved fresh mushrooms
3 medium white new potatoes, cut in 1-inch cubes
1 tablespoon dried parsley
1 teaspoon Lawry's Seasoned Salt

3 pounds beef tenderloin steaks, trimmed of all fat
1 (24-ounce) package frozen stew vegetables, thawed

1. In a 4- or 5-quart dutch oven, melt the butter over medium-high heat. Add the onion and celery and cook over medium heat, stirring, for 3 to 4 minutes.

2. Add the package of pepper sauce mix, the water, bouillon cubes, mushrooms, potatoes, and parsley. Cover and simmer over medium-low heat 1½ hours, or until the potatoes are soft.

3. Sprinkle seasoned salt on the steaks and broil until rare, 4 to 5 minutes on each side, depending on the thickness of the steaks. While the steaks are broiling, add the stew vegetables to the other vegetables and reduce the heat to low.

4. Cut the broiled steaks into stew-meat-size pieces and add to the cooked vegetables, making sure to get all the meat drippings from the broiler pan into the pot. Raise the heat to medium-high for 5 or 6 minutes, stirring frequently.

Serve in large soup bowls, with piping hot hard rolls or thick slices of steaming hot French bread (suitable for royal dunking).

Western Mesquite Broiled Sirloin

This tangy, delicious marinated steak has real Texan flavor without taking all night to get there.

PREPARATION TIME: 1 minute
MARINATING TIME: 30 minutes
BROILING TIME: 6 to 10 minutes to desired doneness
SERVES: 4

1 top sirloin steak (1½ pounds)

MARINADE:
2 cups Lawry's Mesquite Marinade (comes in a 12-ounce bottle)
1 teaspoon coarsely ground pepper
3 cloves garlic, thinly sliced

1. Pierce the steak with a fork and place in a gallon-size reclosable freezer bag. Add the marinade, pepper, and garlic.
2. Seal the bag and refrigerate for at least 30 minutes.
3. Before broiling, bring the steak back to room temperature.
4. Remove the meat from the bag. Reserve the marinade for basting.
5. Basting often, broil for 3 to 5 minutes on each side (3 minutes for rare, 4 for medium-rare, 5 for medium, and longer for wrecked).

This is good served with Country Fair Grilled Walla Wallas (see Index), slices of chilled cucumber and tomato, and corn on the cob.

Fraudulent Lasagna

If you have a great Italian name, feel free to call this fabulous recipe by yours.

PREPARATION TIME: 5 minutes
MICROWAVE TIME: 45 minutes
SERVES: 4 to 6

1 (2 pound, 8-ounce) package Stouffer's Lasagna with Meat & Sauce
1 cup Ripoff Italian Tomato Sauce (see Index)
¼ cup grated Parmesan cheese
½ cup shredded mozzarella cheese
Parsley for garnish

1. Microwave the frozen lasagna on 50 percent power for 30 minutes; then remove film cover and dump partially cooked entrée upside-down into your own square glass or microwave-safe baking dish.

2. Press to fit. Immediately discard Stouffer's container.

3. Pour sauce over the lasagna. (At this point you can feel free to stop calling it Stouffer's Lasagna. It's yours!)

4. Continue microwaving on 50 percent power for 10 minutes. Add the cheeses and cook until they melt. Garnish with sprigs of parsley, or chopped parsley.

Sirloin Tostados

These tostados come alive because of the savory marinated sirloin, the taco sauce, and the fresh guacamole.

PREPARATION TIME: 15 minutes
GRILLING TIME: to desired doneness
SERVES: 4

1 package Lawry's Carne Asada marinade
2 pounds sirloin, sliced ½ inch thick
4 bakery-prepared tostado shells

1 (17-ounce) can Rosarita Refried Beans
6 cups shredded lettuce
1 cup chopped tomato
½ cup chopped onion
¼ cup sliced black olives
1 cup grated Cheddar cheese
1 cup Pace Thick & Chunky Medium Salsa
1 package guacamole mix
2 ripe avocados, mashed
½ cup sour cream

1. In a gallon-size reclosable freezer bag, prepare the marinade according to the package directions. Add the sliced sirloin. Marinate 15 minutes. Remove the meat from the bag.

2. Place the pieces of meat on the grill on a sheet of heavy aluminum foil that has been sprayed with Pam. Pierce the foil with a sharp knife to allow the juices to drain slowly. Grill, turning often, basting one more time with marinade. Grill to the desired doneness.

3. In the tostado shells, layer the beans, lettuce, tomato, onion, olives, cheese, and salsa. Add the steak slices.

4. In a small mixing bowl, prepare the guacamole mix according to the package directions, using the avocados. Top the tostados with guacamole and sour cream.

Braised Beef Tips

This hearty beef dish is a tender, juicy family favorite.

PREPARATION TIME: 10 minutes
MARINATING TIME: 15 minutes
COOKING TIME: 3 hours
SERVES: 6

1 package Lawry's Beef Marinade
3 pounds beef stew meat
1 tablespoon olive oil
1 medium onion, chopped
1 teaspoon Lawry's Garlic Powder Coarse
    Ground with Parsley
1 tablespoon green peppercorns, crushed
3 cups water
1 package Lawry's Brown Gravy Mix

1. Rinse, pierce, and cut the stew meat into bite-size pieces. Pat dry with paper towels.
2. In a gallon-size reclosable freezer bag, mix the marinade according to the package directions. Marinate 15 minutes.
3. In a heavy kettle, heat the olive oil. Sauté the onion until it softens. Remove the meat from the marinade (discard marinade), add it to the onions, and brown. Season with garlic powder and pepper.
4. Add 3 cups water. Simmer over medium heat for 1 hour. Reduce the heat to low and simmer 2 more hours. Check the liquid level periodically to make sure the meat is covered.
5. Mix the brown gravy according to the package directions. Add to the meat, stirring until the sauce thickens.

Good served with mashed potatoes or rice and steamed green beans.

Hungry Man in a Blanket

Because of the tender, flaky blanket, this delicious recipe stretches two frozen dinners into enough for four! And it's fancy enough for company.

PREPARATION TIME: 8 minutes
COOKING TIME: 25 minutes
SERVES: 4

1 sheet Pepperidge Farm frozen Puff Pastry,
    thawed 20 minutes

2 (10½-ounce) Hungry Man Frozen
   Dinners (turkey), thawed in the refrigerator overnight
¼ cup minced onion

1. On a floured pastry board, cut the pastry sheet in half and roll each half into a 12-inch square.
2. In the middle of each sheet of pastry, place the turkey portion of the Hungry Man dinner turkey side down, stuffing side up. Divide the potato portion in half in order to cover the entrée portion, which is twice as long as the potatoes. Layer the peas and onion over the potatoes. Wrap the Hungry Man by bringing up the ends of the pastry and folding over once (the same way you would wrap a sandwich in waxpaper). Dab ¼ teaspoon water along the inside edges of the open ends of pastry and press closed with fork to seal tightly.
3. Place packets on a cookie sheet and bake in a 400-degree oven for 25 minutes.
4. Warm dessert portions of the frozen dinners in the microwave and serve with vanilla ice cream.

Great served with Scrumptious and Simply Simple Spinach Salad (see Index).

Spooky Tortilla Pie

From Pam

When you were a kid, did you ever go to a Halloween party and see spiders, flies, and lizards floating on the surface of the punch? I remember the first time I saw a punch bowl with the little plastic animals bobbing around among the ice cubes, because I liked it very much. It made such an impression on me that when I grew up and became a mother I made sure my kids' parties not only had swamp punch, but ALL the party treats had sort of a Steven Spielberg flair. This tortilla pie doesn't have fake animals in it, but it will definitely get everyone's attention!

Just for fun, or to teach a valuable life lesson (don't judge a book by its cover), serve this muck-ugly (on purpose) but absolutely fabulous-tasting tortilla pie.

PREPARATION TIME: 12 minutes
COOKING TIME: 20 minutes
SERVES: 4

1 pound ground beef
8 drops green food coloring

3 drops blue food coloring
1/4 teaspoon vinegar
1/2 cup chopped onion
1 (12-ounce) jar salsa (mild to medium,
    depending on your taste)
1/2 teaspoon Lawry's Seasoned Salt
1/2 teaspoon Lawry's Garlic Powder Coarse
    Ground with Parsley
2 tablespoons Presti's Taco
    Seasoning
3 large flour tortillas
1 cup Crispy, Crumby, Counterfeit Cover-
    up (see Index)
Salt and freshly ground pepper

1. In a medium-size skillet, fry the ground beef. Drain off the fat. Add 3 drops of the green food coloring to the meat.
2. In a medium bowl, add the blue food coloring and vinegar to the onion. As soon as the onion has turned bright blue, add the salsa, seasoned salt, onion, remaining green food coloring, garlic, and taco seasoning. Add to ground beef and simmer over medium heat for 5 minutes.
3. Place a tortilla on the bottom of a 10-inch pie pan sprayed with Pam No Stick Cooking Spray. Cut the other 2 tortillas into 4 equal triangles and arrange (points down) to cover the sides.
4. Pour the meat mixture into the pie pan.

Top with crumb topping and bake in a 375-degree oven for 15 minutes.

Tip: For an extra-provocative way to serve raw onion and grated cheese with this dish, put both raw onion and cheese in a quart-size reclosable bag, add 4 drops of blue food coloring, and shake well.

Mom's Numskull Turkey Casserole

From Peggy

The other day, Mom came over with a little dish covered with Saran Wrap and said, "Peg, taste this casserole and see if you think it's any good. I made it for Dad and he went nuts over it. If you don't like it you won't hurt my feelings, but I thought you might want to put it in your book." It was delicious!

After she saw that I loved it, she reached into her purse and pulled out a 3 × 5 card with the recipe written on it. I told her we'd definitely use it, but when I started to put it into the computer, I realized that we had a huge problem. Mom cooks by instinct, the way Granny did and

Pam and I do. We had to learn how to explain our recipes more clearly, so that you could understand exactly what we're doing. Just as Mom can't read music but can sing four-part harmony, she can't write recipes but she's a fabulous cook. I called her for more information.

"It says here 'leftover chicken or turkey.' Which did you use?"

"Turkey. But chicken would be just as good, don't you think?"

"Yeah, but let's just say turkey."

"Yeah."

"Was it cooked and cut up?"

"Yeah, it was the leftovers from Sunday's roast turkey."

"How many cups?"

"I didn't measure. But you know, whatever would be left from the breast of about a ten-pound turkey. Dad and I can't eat as much as we used to. I can remember when I'd cook a bird as big as a small child and there wouldn't be one scrap left. Remember that woman, oh you know who I mean, the one who always walks around the mall in those pants they're all wearing . . . what do you call 'em . . . you know what I'm talking about . . . they're real tight and they go into your shoes . . . stirrup pants . . . anyway what's her name . . . she's married to that old guy who always scratched himself when

he talked to you . . . you know, he was on the school board, what was his name . . . I can't think of it . . . anyway I ran into her at the Food Barn and she said THEY can't eat the way they used to either—"

"Mom?"

"Yeah."

"What do you think—a couple of cups?"

"Huh?"

"For the casserole, do you think a couple of cups of turkey would be about right?"

"Yeah. Dad, who's that woman we ran into over at the store the other day? You used to deliver stove oil to 'em when they lived over there where the new fire station is? DAD!! He can't hear."

"Now it says, 'One can of cream of chicken or cream of mushroom soup (undiluted).' Which one did you use?"

"Cream of mushroom, but cream of chicken would be good too, don't you think? Glenda Featherly! That's who I was trying to think of! DAD, GLENDA FEATHERLY!"

We went through what she had written and she told me what she meant by it. I asked her what size casserole dish; she said "just a regular one." We discussed seasoning and she said "just the regular seasoning." I asked about the bread cubes and the temperature and time in the oven. She said it'd depend on my oven and I should just cook it, "You know, till it's done." When I asked her if we should tell you to spray the casserole dish with Pam, she said, "Oh don't you think any numskull would know that?"

I had just hung up from talking to my son Jeff (from his apartment at the University of Washington) before I called Mom. He had called to ask me what went wrong with his dinner. "I made Grama's meatloaf like she told me to but it didn't look anything like hers. It wouldn't even come out of the pan."

Now we need you to know that Jeff is no NUMSKULL! In fact he'd bury my mom in a single round of *Jeopardy!* Unfortunately, he doesn't have the Gullickson (our mother's family name) gift of natural cooking instinct, so she'd kill him with the recipe she handed me. Anyway, here is Mom's delicious, user-friendly recipe for numskulls as well as intellectuals. (It's a recipe for turkey, not numskulls and intellectuals, but I'm sure you got that.)

This is so good you'll be up in the middle of the night to sneak leftovers. The next day when your mate rummages through the refrigerator and asks what happened to the rest of the dinner, tell him the dog ate it.

PREPARATION TIME: 15 minutes
COOKING TIME: 45 minutes
SERVES: 4

2 cups cooked and cubed turkey breast
1 (10½-ounce) can Campbell's Condensed Cream of Mushroom Soup
1 cup small-curd low-fat cottage cheese
2 stalks celery, coarsely chopped
½ medium onion, finely chopped
1 (8-ounce) can mushroom stems and pieces, in half their liquid
1 (8-ounce) can sliced water chestnuts, drained
½ teaspoon Lawry's Seasoned LITE Salt
Pepper
½ cup Pepperidge Farm Herb Seasoned Stuffing

1. In a large mixing bowl, mix together the turkey, soup, cottage cheese, celery, onion, mushrooms, water chestnuts, Lawry's, and pepper.
2. Pour into a 1½-quart casserole dish that has been sprayed with Pam.
3. Sprinkle the top with dry stuffing crumbs. Cover with foil. Bake in a 350-degree oven for 45 minutes.

Tip: Lawry's Seasoned LITE Salt is used in this recipe because Mom and Dad are supposed to be very careful of their salt intake. It's a good alternative to the old standby and can be substituted in all of our recipes if necessary.

Deli-icious Turkey Divan

From Peggy

I made up this recipe because I was stuck with a bunch of sliced deli turkey that I bought from a membership-type discount store we call "Cramco." (It's really called Costco but whenever we shop there, we buy too much stuff and have to cram it into the car to get it home.) Anyway, I bought a package of deli turkey that could feed an aircraft carrier full of hungry sailors. When the five of us got sick of sandwiches, I had to use up the sliced poultry another way before it became foul. The results were delicious.

This one-dish meal looks and tastes as if you'd put a lot of time and effort into it. The combination of moist stuffing, fresh broccoli, and tender slices of turkey is wonderful.

PREPARATION TIME: 10 minutes
BAKING TIME: 30 minutes
SERVES: 6

2   cups The Incredible Crouton (see Index)
1   small onion, thinly sliced
1   (10½-ounce) can Campbell's Condensed
     Cream of Chicken Soup
½   cup sour cream
2   chicken-flavored bouillon cubes
1   cup boiling water
1½ pounds deli turkey (about 12 slices)
2   cups fresh broccoli florets
½   teaspoon Lawry's Seasoned Salt
White pepper
1½ cups grated Cheddar cheese

1. Place the croutons in the bottom of an oblong baking dish. (These will automatically become stuffing in the baking process.)
2. Cover the cubes with the slices of onion.
3. In a small bowl, mix up a sauce using the soup, sour cream, and bouillon cubes that have been dissolved in the hot water. Pour half of the sauce over the stuffing in the baking dish.
4. Top with a layer of turkey slices and a layer of broccoli. Sprinkle with seasoning to taste. Add another layer of succulent fowl.

5. Pour the rest of the sauce over the top of the turkey. Cover the baking dish. Bake in a 350-degree oven for 20 minutes.
6. Remove the cover. Sprinkle the top with grated cheese; cover again and bake another ten minutes, or until the cheese melts.

Good served with a green salad.

Tip: As an alternative to homemade croutons, use 2 cups of Pepperidge Farm Herb Seasoned Stuffing.

Krafty Garlic Chicken and Macaroni Salad Dinner

No one will ever know that most of this tasty dinner came from a box! The fresh chicken breasts are tender and so delicious cooked in the creamy garlic cheese sauce. The pasta, with the variety of mixed vegetables, is bright, colorful, and luscious.

PREPARATION TIME: 10 minutes
COOKING TIME: 26 minutes
SERVES: 4

1 (7¼-ounce) box Kraft Macaroni and Cheese
1 tablespoon olive oil
4 boneless chicken breast halves, skinned
1 cup buttermilk
½ teaspoon Lawry's Garlic Powder Coarse Ground with Parsley
2 drops red food coloring
1 drop blue food coloring
2 cups frozen mixed vegetables, thawed
3 tablespoons Catalina Dressing (or your favorite salad dressing)
Salt and freshly ground pepper

1. In a 2-quart kettle, boil the macaroni according to the package directions. Drain and cool.
2. In a medium skillet, heat the oil over medium-high heat. Brown the chicken on both sides (about 3 minutes on each side). Remove from heat.
3. In a small bowl, mix the buttermilk, garlic, the dry package of cheese sauce from the Kraft package, and food coloring drops. (You are going for a nice brown color, rather than the "give-away" orange

of Kraft Macaroni and Cheese.) Pour over the chicken, cover, and simmer over medium-low heat for 20 minutes, turning the chicken occasionally.

4. In a food processor, finely chop the mixed vegetables. Add to the cooked macaroni and toss with the salad dressing. Season with salt and pepper.

Crazy Ed's Parmesan Chicken Dijon

Just because Ed isn't on the main road doesn't mean he isn't a great cook. His delicious, crispy, tangy chicken entrée is far removed from traditional fare. It will be so popular with your family that you may want to double or even triple the recipe.

PREPARATION TIME: 15 minutes
COOKING TIME: 45 minutes
SERVES: 8

½ cup (1 stick) butter or margarine
3 tablespoons Dijon-style mustard
1½ teaspoons Lawry's Garlic Powder Coarse Ground with Parsley
2 tablespoons Lea & Perrins Worcestershire Sauce
1 teaspoon Lawry's Seasoned Salt
2 cups grated Parmesan cheese
1½ cups bread crumbs
8 boneless chicken breast halves (about 5 ounces each)

1. In a 9-inch glass pie plate, melt the butter in the microwave. Add the mustard, garlic, Worcestershire sauce, and seasoned salt. Mix thoroughly.

2. In a small bowl, mix 1½ cups of the cheese with the bread crumbs.

3. Dip each breast half in butter mixture; roll into a ball and coat with the cheese and crumb mixture.

4. In a shallow baking dish, place the bundles close together. Sprinkle the remaining ½ cup cheese over the tops of the bundles. Bake in a 375-degree oven for 45 minutes.

Tip: This recipe freezes well, uncooked. You could double it and freeze half. When you are ready to use the half you froze, thaw completely before baking.

Peggy's Chicken Rockefeller

From Peggy

I don't know how the Rockefellers became associated with oysters. John Davison Rockefeller was born in Richmond, New York, the son of a peddler. When he was fourteen, his family moved to Cleveland, Ohio, where he attended high school. He

started work at sixteen as a clerk in a small produce firm. He then formed a partner ship in a grain commission house. With the profits from the business, Rockefeller entered the oil business at twenty-three. Because of his success in the oil fields, he was able to buy many things, among which was his coveted beach property.

I think that Oysters Rockefeller made their debut when John Jr. and his family were summering at the shore, enjoying the perks of being kin to tycoons. The little tycoonets, not knowing that they were rich, gathered a bunch of the oyster shells and took them up to the house to show them to their folks. I imagine that Mother Rockefeller (trying to bring the family back to the basics) had just come in from the garden with a bunch of produce when the little fellers came into the kitchen dragging a sack of oysters.

Nelson probably said, "Mom, look what we found on the beach, can we eat 'em!?" and she said, "But of course. I'll cook them for you, but only if you'll promise to eat your spinach." They agreed and then she had to figure out a way to throw off the powerful taste of spinach that all kids hate. Since they'd been all over the world collecting fine wines and liqueurs, the Rockefellers had a well-stocked bar. While she was thinking about fixing dinner, she poured herself a touch of Pernod. After a few sips, it hit her! "The kids love licorice and the licorice-tasting Pernod would be a flavor just powerful enough to take over the spinach." (John was an oyster man from Harvard so he'd love anything she did with them. It was the kids she was worried about.)

The sensory gratification that her recipe represented gained her the status she now enjoys in fine restaurants around the world. The wonderful combination of taste, texture, look, and smell makes anything "Rockefeller" unforgettable.

Ring, ring, ring.

"Hello?"

"Sissy? I know where oysters Rockefeller came from."

"Huh? I just finished writing what I thought probably happened and I'm happy with it."

"Well, do you want to know the truth?"

"Humph . . . yeah, sure."

"OK, here's what happened. This restaurant owner in New Orleans, named Antoine, had a big reputation for serving fine food."

"Uh-huh."

"Yeah, and guess what? One day he ran out of snails (they were on the appetizer menu) so he panicked and he told his son to go down to the docks and get whatever he could find and they'd figure out what to do with what he got later. So, Antoine's son, we'll call him Todd, could only get a sack of oysters with a bunch of seaweed hanging off 'em. When Todd gave the sack to Antoine, the old entrepreneur had to pull himself together. He scraped the seaweed off the shells and got busy in the kitchen."

"Schwoooo—"

"Yeah. Then he crossed the snails off the menu and wrote in 'Oysters Rockefeller.' He thought of the richest name he could and tacked it onto the oysters so his customers would think they were worth the price he was charging. I guess restaurants everywhere have been trying to reconcoct the original recipe using spinach, but it's not quite the same as the green stuff he put on top of his oysters."

"Humph—"

"Yeah, and Antoine won't tell his secret."

"I'll bet that's 'cause old Antoine was embarrassed. I'll bet he used the seaweed hanging off the oyster shells for the spinachy stuff and he just won't address it. Anytime a chef has to say something's a secret it's because the truth's embarrassing."

"Sissy, speaking about the truth, I made up some of that story."

"Yeah, I know, but don't tell me what part, I liked it the way it was."

If you've ever had oysters Rockefeller and you liked them, then picture chicken in the place of the oysters and you've got this elegant dish.

PREPARATION TIME: 15 minutes
BAKING TIME: 40 minutes
SERVES: 6

½ cup light sour cream
1 package onion soup mix
1 cup shredded Cheddar cheese
1 (10-ounce package) frozen spinach, thawed, then squeezed to death
½ teaspoon Chinese-style five-spice powder
½ teaspoon Lawry's Garlic Powder Coarse Ground with Parsley
3 tablespoons chopped fresh parsley
2 cups chicken stock
6 chicken breast halves, skinned, boned, and flattened

1. In a large bowl, mix the sour cream, soup mix, cheese, spinach, five-spice powder, garlic, and fresh parsley.
2. Loosen the mixture with some of the chicken stock. (We used to make mud pies with grass, dirt, and dandelions, adding a smidgen of water until it looked like and had the same consistency that this mixture should have. It should be like a thick, fresh, strawberry milkshake.)
3. Place some of the spinach mixture along the long side of each flattened breast. Roll up starting on a long side and wrap very loosely in foil boatlike packages to allow liquid to enter during the baking time.
4. Place the partially open packages in a baking dish and pour the remaining chicken stock over the top. Bake in a 350-degree oven for 35 to 40 minutes.

Tip: If you don't have homemade chicken stock on hand, substitute a 10½-ounce can of chicken broth and enough water to make 2 cups of liquid. The Chinese-style five-spice powder gives the dish the licorice flavor of anisette or Pernod. Leave it out if you don't like the taste.

Chicken Hollandaise

PREPARATION TIME: 5 minutes
COOKING TIME: 6 to 8 hours
SERVES: 4 to 5

1 whole chicken, skinned and cut up
1 cup chicken stock
1 package Hollandaise Sauce Blend from
    the McCormick Collection
1 (8-ounce) package Philadelphia Brand
    Cream Cheese
2 cups fettuccine, cooked

1. In a crockery cooker or covered baking dish, place the chicken pieces, chicken stock, and hollandaise sauce.
2. Cook on low setting or in a 250-degree oven for 6 to 8 hours.
3. At dinner time, cook the fettuccine according to the package directions and while it's boiling, remove the chicken from the pot and add the cream cheese to the liquid in the pot. Stir until melted. Put the chicken on a bed of fettuccine and pour the sauce over the chicken.

Chicken Sauté with Wild Mushroom Sauce

A unique and satisfying recipe, rich with wild mushrooms, wine, and a blend of herbs and spices.

PREPARATION TIME: 5 minutes
COOKING TIME: 20 minutes
SERVES: 4

2 tablespoons butter
1 pound chicken cutlets
1/4 cup chopped onion
1 cup water
1/2 cup milk
1 package Knorr Cream of Wild Mushroom
    Soupmix

1. In a large skillet, melt the butter over medium-high heat. Add the chicken cutlets. Sauté 5 minutes. Remove from the skillet.
2. To the same skillet, add the onion. Sauté 2 minutes.
3. Stir in the water, milk, and soup mix. Stirring constantly, bring to a boil. Return the chicken to the skillet. Reduce the heat to low; simmer 10 minutes.

Hudson's Bay Company Breast of Chicken

We live just a few miles from a very historic site called Fort Vancouver. The spot is riddled with arrowheads and crawling with archaeologists. This recipe isn't named after the famous British trading firm that set up business at Fort Vancouver on the Columbia River. Instead, it's named after the high school here in Vancouver, which was named after the trading company. The reason we named it after Hudson's Bay High School is probably the same reason they named the high school after the trading company. We like the name. Besides, the name Company Chicken doesn't quite do it for us.

This quick and delicious dish stars Philadelphia Brand Cream Cheese and fresh parsley. Prepare ahead and store in the refrigerator for up to two days before using.

PREPARATION TIME: 10 minutes
COOKING TIME: 25 minutes
SERVES: 8

8 boneless chicken breast halves, skinned
1 teaspoon Lawry's Seasoned Salt
5 tablespoons butter or margarine
1 large onion, finely chopped
1/4 pound mushrooms, sliced
2 tablespoons chopped fresh parsley

1 (17¼-ounce) package Pepperidge Farm frozen Puff Pastry Sheets, thawed 20 minutes
1 (8-ounce) package Philadelphia Brand Cream Cheese
2 tablespoons Dijon-style mustard

1. Preheat the oven to 375 degrees. Sprinkle the chicken with seasoned salt.
2. In a medium skillet, brown the chicken in 3 tablespoons of the butter over medium heat. Remove the chicken and set aside. To the same skillet, add the remaining 2 tablespoons butter, the onion, and mushrooms and sauté until tender and the liquid has evaporated. Stir in the parsley.
3. On a lightly floured surface, roll each puff pastry sheet into a 14-inch square; cut each square into four 7-inch squares.
4. In a small bowl, combine the cream cheese with the mustard and spread over the chicken breasts. Spread each pastry square with 2 tablespoons of the mushroom mixture. Top each with a chicken breast. Brush the edges of the pastry with water and wrap the pastry around the chicken, pressing the edges to seal. Place seam side down on baking sheet. Bake 25 minutes, or until puffed and golden brown.

Chicken Breasts in Sweet and Sour Winter Sauce

From Pam

The February issue of a woman's magazine listed "101 Romantic Things to Do with Your Husband." The one that struck my fanciful heart was number 43: "Have a candlelight picnic." Since it was winter when I got the idea (and I'm impulsive), it's no wonder my candlelight picnic was a WINTER one. I pulled the picnic table out of storage and rolled it, on its two wooden wheels, over the meadow behind our house to a pastoral picnic spot in the woods overlooking Salmon Creek. Out of sight of our house or any neighbors, I spread my red-and-white-checkered tablecloth and set a scene straight out of a LaVyrle Spencer novel. In the middle of the table, I put two red tapers in silver candlestick holders on either side of a Christmas Poinsettia that was trying to hold on to its last holiday breath.

I put the ice chest, packed with the hot food, into the wheelbarrow along with a produce box holding the salad, bread, and pie, and a boom box owned by my then teenage daughter, Joanna. (I moved the booming station from rock to classical.) I headed over the hill into the blackness of the night. Thanks to Chelsea Marie, my trusty bassett hound, who sniffed our way, we made it to the spot with only minor injuries. I lit the candles and headed back to the house to get my mate.

Terry was watching the six o'clock news. He'd already changed clothes from work and was settled in the recliner in his favorite sweat shirt, jeans, and house slippers. He didn't suspect a thing.

"Terry, dinner is ready, but you have to put on different shoes."

I wish you could have seen the look he gave me. I might as well have said, "Terry, dinner is ready, but you need to put on your combat gear for another stint in Vietnam."

As we walked through the meadow, this time with a flashlight, we looked up and gazed at the brilliant stars, a sight we would have missed that night if we had eaten in the house. The evening was everything I imagined it to be. We ended up staying out there for two hours, talking about everything from Bigfoot to Casper, the friendly ghost.

I recommend a candlelight picnic, but I caution you to read Peggy's experience with Danny before you try to pull off this romantic meal idea.

From Peggy

A candlelight picnic ... ah, how special it sounded when my sister recounted the fabulous evening she and Terry had enjoyed. Danny and I are approaching three decades of marriage and I'm a firm believer in trying new things to keep the marriage fresh. "OK," I thought, "just because we aren't exactly newlyweds doesn't mean there isn't a fire some place ... let's go for it!"

Our candlelight picnic memory was made the very next Saturday. Allyson spent the night with Peggy Ann (my namesake niece) and before Danny came home from work, the steamy scene was set.

I'm not a woods person (thanks to my older sister who played snake tricks on me), so despite the fact that we live overlooking a wildlife refuge and I could have hauled the table down to the lake, my picnic took place on our lower deck. It's very secluded and beautiful down there. Perched at the top of a canyon, the deck surrounds an in-ground pool that Danny keeps sparkling throughout the year. Our picnic was going to be Robin Leach–like and nothing could wreck the elegant, resorty mood I'd created.

I knew Danny would reject the idea of eating outside in the middle of winter if I came right out and asked him to. I also know he hates surprises. More than that, he hates having to do things just because my sister tells me we ought to.

This new idea of hers had been Terry-tested and seemed to be a winner, so I proceeded with my plan. My outdoor table setting was beautiful. A chaise longue let down to the max with a blanket thrown over it made an inviting seat for two. The other let-down chaise, placed in front of the seat, was draped with an ivory tablecloth that transformed the webbed eyesore into a lovely place to dine. Candles, china, crystal ... the works, and everything was ready ... except for one detail. I threw down a camping mat and two zipped-together sleeping bags so that we could watch the after-dinner picnic stars without neck strain.

To make a long story less graphic, the only thing that kept Danny on the deck through dinner was the lure of the sleeping bags. Yes, they started out to be an enticement, but in the end they were the key to survival. On the day of my candlelight picnic, Washington State took a record dive in temperature from unseasonably mild at six o'clock to uncommonly frigid at seven. While we were eating, we felt the subtle yet remarkable drop. Before we knew it, the lettuce in the salad looked as if it had been in the crisper too long, the candles sank, the chicken breasts were stiff, the wineglasses were frosted, and the dew on the deck turned white.

We jumped into the sleeping bags to watch the winter's starry sky. We cuddled close together, not to be romantic but to try to warm up. We didn't talk about love; we talked about the homeless who were in sleeping bags just as we were, only huddled together under the Burnside Bridge. We didn't even kiss. If either one of us moved, it broke the seal on the sleeping bags and the freezing night air snuck in. Too cold to run for the house, we stayed outside until early morning. I think we'll try it again in the summer if we're still married. Danny said, "Tell your sister thanks again."

When it's cold outside, people pay money to participate in outdoor winter sports. Why not show off in front of a Weber Kettle barbecue rather than on the slopes? Bundling up with a significant for a frosty barbecue under a frozen, starry sky can be just as exhilarating as white powder, and you won't end up on crutches. You might get frostbite, but you won't end up in a cast!

This is a deliciously different sweet and sour twist on a sauce that you can use on pork or chicken on the barbecue.

PREPARATION TIME: 5 minutes
COOKING TIME: 5 minutes
GRILLING TIME: 30 minutes
SERVES: 4

4 *chicken breast halves, skinned and boned*
½ *teaspoon Lawry's Seasoned Salt*
½ *teaspoon Lawry's Garlic Powder Coarse*
    Ground with Parsley

FOR SAUCE:
½ *cup rice wine vinegar*
½ *cup packed brown sugar*
½ *cup drained crushed pineapple*
¼ *cup finely chopped onion*
1 *teaspoon Lawry's Garlic Powder Coarse*
    Ground with Parsley
¼ *cup cooking sherry or white wine*

1 tablespoon soy sauce
1 teaspoon grated fresh gingerroot
2 tablespoons water
1 tablespoon cornstarch

1. Put a sheet of heavy aluminum foil that has been sprayed with Pam on a hot barbecue grill. With a sharp knife, make several ½-inch slices in the foil, about 2 inches apart, to allow the juices to drain and create a slight smoky flavor during cooking.
2. Sprinkle the chicken breasts with seasonings and place them on the grill for 10 minutes, turning often.

To make the sauce:
1. In a medium saucepan, heat the vinegar, brown sugar, pineapple, onion, garlic powder, sherry, soy sauce, and gingerroot until the mixture bubbles and the onions soften.
2. In a small measuring cup, mix together the water and cornstarch and add to the sauce to thicken. Continue cooking until the sauce becomes transparent.
3. Pour half the sauce over the chicken to smother the breasts during the last 20 minutes of barbecuing. Turn the breasts often, brushing with the remaining sauce.

Good served with steamed rice.

Tip: If you can't get fresh gingerroot, postpone this recipe until you can.

Blue Cheese Chicken Italiano

Only a fool would turn a piece of pizza upside down, because all the stuff would fall off it. That's why no one has ever seen the underside of a piece of pizza. When you serve Blue Cheese Chicken Italiano you will actually be premiering the underside of a Totino's Party Pizza. It's very pretty. It looks a little like a soda cracker with a puffy surface and little holes in a geometric design. When you cover this zesty chicken entrée with the mystery top, even Columbo wouldn't be able to figure out what has made the fabulous pastry topping or what has given this dish its tasty assortment of mushrooms, meats, and cheeses.

Quick, easy, delicious, and very SNEAKY!

PREPARATION TIME: 10 minutes
COOKING TIME: 55 minutes
SERVES: 4

3 boneless, skinless chicken breast halves
    (about 5 ounces each)
1 (10¾-ounce) can Campbell's Cream of
    Mushroom Soup
¼ cup crumbled blue cheese
¼ cup sour cream
2 whole cloves garlic
Salt and pepper
1 (10.9-ounce) Totino's Party Pizza
½ cup shredded mozzarella cheese

1. Pound the chicken breasts to flatten, and place them in bottom of a buttered 11-inch pie plate. Smear half the can of soup on the breasts.
2. In a blender, blend the other half of the canned soup with the blue cheese, sour cream, and garlic. Pour over the chicken breasts in the pie plate. Add salt and pepper.
3. Place the frozen pizza upside down on the chicken; cover with foil and bake in a 375-degree oven for 45 minutes. Remove the foil, sprinkle with the cheese, and continue baking for 10 more minutes, until the cheese melts.

Tip: We suggest using Totino's "Combination" or one of its three terrific new party pizzas, any of which are excellent: Zesty Italiano, Supreme, or Three Meat. Sounds like a commercial—it's not. The new party pizzas are a little larger than the originals, so cut around the edge to fit the pie plate.

Note: It's very important to cover this dish with foil so the pizza crust can soak up the delicious sauce and stay tender during cooking. The crust will get crisp when the foil is removed and the dish bakes for 10 more minutes.

Chicken Rapture Under Wraps

PREPARATION TIME: 14 minutes
COOKING TIME: 25 minutes
SERVES: 4

4 boneless chicken breast halves, skinned
2 tablespoons butter or margarine
1 (10-ounce) package frozen creamed
    spinach, thawed

¼ cup grated Parmesan cheese
¼ cup chopped roasted cashews
½ teaspoon Lawry's Garlic Powder Coarse
    Ground with Parsley
½ teaspoon Lawry's Seasoned Salt
1 sheet Pepperidge Farm frozen Puff Pastry,
    thawed 20 minutes
Salt and fresh ground pepper

1. In a medium skillet, brown the chicken breasts in butter over medium-high heat. Set aside.
2. In a small bowl, combine the spinach, cheese, nuts, garlic, seasoned salt, salt, and pepper.
3. Roll the pastry on a lightly floured surface to a 14-inch square; cut the square into four 7-inch squares. Spoon the spinach mixture into the center of each square. Top with the chicken breasts. Wrap the pastry to enclose the chicken. Seal. Place the packets seam side down on an ungreased baking sheet.
4. Bake in a 375-degree oven for 20 minutes, or until golden brown.

Lemon Chicken San Francisco Treat

We have served this lovely chicken and rice entrée to an authentic gourmet who raved about the fabulous flavor and presentation. She wanted the recipe. We said we'd try to get permission from "the family" to give it to her.

These chicken breasts look beautiful, and steamed to tenderness along with the broccoli florets, they make a colorful, nutritious main dish.

PREPARATION TIME: 10 minutes
COOKING TIME: 30 minutes
SERVES: 6

6   chicken breast halves, skinned and
      boned
¼   cup flour
2   tablespoons olive oil
6   tablespoons (¾ stick) margarine
3   tablespoons fresh lemon juice
2   tablespoons chopped parsley, plus addi-
      tional for garnish
2   tablespoons chopped green onion

1 (6.9-ounce) package Rice-A-Roni,
     Chicken Flavor
2½ cups hot water
1½ cups fresh broccoli florets
3   tablespoons grated Parmesan cheese

1. In a reclosable freezer bag, shake the chicken breasts in flour.
2. In a large skillet, heat the oil and 4 tablespoons (½ stick) margarine over medium-high heat. Add the floured chicken. Cook 5 minutes on each side. Remove from the skillet and set aside.
3. In the same skillet, stir the lemon juice and parsley into the oil-margarine mixture. Pour over the chicken. Remove to a rimmed plate and keep warm.
4. In the same skillet, prepare the Rice-A-Roni mix, adding the remaining 2 tablespoons margarine and hot water as the package directs. Stir in the broccoli after the rice has simmered 15 minutes. Top with the chicken covered with parsley-lemon sauce. Sprinkle with cheese.

Good served with green salad and sourdough bread.

Tip: Transfer this skillet meal into a pretty chafing dish to make an elegant presentation. Garnish with fresh parsley.

Shoplifted Chicken Supreme

Pay for the Stouffer's Lean Cuisines, but steal all the credit for the incredible taste that will come out of your kitchen. This is so delicious, your family will truly think you spent at least an hour fixing dinner. They should help with the dishes after this one.

PREPARATION TIME: 5 minutes
COOKING TIME: 30 minutes
SERVES: 4

1 cup chicken stock
1 tablespoon cornstarch
1 can Campbell's Cream of Chicken Soup
1 cup grated Cheddar cheese
2 cups pasta of your choice, cooked al dente
    (sort of cooked)
2 (8½-ounce) packages Stouffer's Lean
    Cuisine Glazed Chicken
1 cup Crispy, Crumby, Counterfeit Cover-up
    (see Index)

1. In a small bowl, combine the chicken stock, cornstarch, cream soup, and cheese.
2. Lightly butter a medium-size baking dish. Cover the bottom of dish with pasta. Remove the frozen glazed chicken servings from the cardboard containers and arrange on top of the pasta. Pour the cream soup mixture over the glazed chicken.
3. Bake at 350 degrees for 25 minutes. Add the crumb topping and return to the oven until the topping is browned, about 5 minutes.

Skinny Hawaiian Chicken à L'orange

Your family will love these chicken tenderloins simmered in a creamy sauce with the subtle tastes of pineapple and orange, and topped with a crispy potato crust.

PREPARATION TIME: 7 minutes
COOKING TIME: 35 minutes
SERVES: 4 Lean Cuisines

3 (9-ounce) packages Stouffer's Lean Cuisine Chicken à l'Orange
2 stalks celery
1/2 cup chopped onion
1/2 cup chopped green pepper
1 whole clove garlic
1 (6-ounce) jar Gerber's Hawaiian Delight Baby Food (3rd foods variety)
1 (3-ounce) package Philadelphia Brand Cream Cheese
1/2 cup water
2 teaspoons cornstarch
1/2 teaspoon Lawry's Seasoned Salt
1 (12-ounce) package OreIda Hash Browns
1/2 cup Crispy, Crumby, Counterfeit Cover-up (optional; see Index)

1. In the bottom of a medium-size square baking dish sprayed with Pam, place the Lean Cuisines broken into small pieces (about the size of an infant's fist).
2. In a food processor, chop the celery, onion, green pepper, and garlic. Distribute evenly over the chicken.
3. Without cleaning the food processor, blend the baby food, cream cheese, water, cornstarch, and seasoned salt. Pour over the chicken.
4. Top with the hash browns. Bake in a 375-degree oven for 35 minutes.

5. If you want to disguise the familiar look of hash brown patties, remove the dish from the oven after baking, spread the patties around with a fork, and sprinkle on ½ cup of Crispy, Crumby, Counterfeit Cover-up. Return to the oven for five minutes.

Borderline Chicken Amarillo

This unique blend of bell peppers, garlic, chile peppers, herbs, and spices will give an "all-the-way-through" southwestern flavor in minutes.

PREPARATION TIME: 5 minutes
MARINATE: 15 minutes
GRILLING TIME: 40 minutes
SERVES: 6

2½ pounds Tyson Boneless, Skinless Thigh
     Portions
1   package Lawry's Southwest Chicken
     Marinade
½   cup water
¼   cup orange juice
⅛   teaspoon cayenne pepper
1   teaspoon Lawry's Garlic Powder Coarse
     Ground with Parsley

1. Rinse and pierce the pieces of chicken with a fork. Pat dry with paper towels.
2. In a gallon-size reclosable freezer bag, mix the Lawry's marinade, water, orange juice, pepper, and garlic.
3. Place the chicken in the bag and marinate for 15 minutes.
4. Put a sheet of heavy aluminum foil that has been sprayed with Pam on a hot barbecue grill. With a sharp knife, make several ½-inch slices in the foil about 2 inches apart to allow the juices to drain to create a slight smoky flavor during cooking.
5. Barbecue the chicken for about 30 to 40 minutes, turning often and basting with the remaining marinade in the bag.

Baked Chicken Bundles

The crusty coating makes the outside of this chicken dish crispy while the moist rice and vermicelli stuffing on the inside keeps the bundles juicy while baking.

PREPARATION TIME: 20 minutes
BAKING TIME: 45 to 50 minutes
SERVES: 8

1   (5-ounce) package Rice-A-Roni Chicken
      & Mushroom Flavor
2   tablespoons margarine
1²⁄₃ cups hot water
¼   cup milk, plus additional for dipping
      chicken bundles
8   chicken breast halves, skinned and boned
½   cup Progresso Italian Style Bread Crumbs
¼   cup (½ stick) margarine, melted
¼   teaspoon thyme
⅛   teaspoon pepper

1. In a large skillet, prepare the Rice-A-Roni mix as the package directs using the margarine, water, and milk.
2. Pound the chicken breast halves to ¼-inch thickness.
3. Divide the Rice-A-Roni equally, placing a portion on each chicken breast half. Roll up the chicken from a long side to enclose the filling completely. Secure with wooden picks.
4. Dip the chicken bundles into milk, then roll them in bread crumbs. Place in a 9 × 13-inch baking dish.
5. In a small bowl, combine the melted margarine, thyme, and pepper; drizzle over the chicken. In a 375-degree oven, bake 45 to 50 minutes, or until light golden brown. Remove the wooden picks before serving.

Tips: Soak the wooden picks in water for a few minutes so they will be easy to pull out when the chicken is cooked.

Any good blend of Italian seasoning may be substituted for the thyme.

Wiener Schnitzel Michelin

When you bite into this crispy, succulent entrée, you are going to think you have died and gone to Germany. We've taken all the work out of hammering the pork loins until they are thin.

PREPARATION TIME: 10 minutes
COOKING TIME: 6 minutes
SERVES: 4

4 boneless pork loins, each 1 inch thick
¼ cup fresh lemon juice
1 teaspoon Lawry's Garlic Powder Coarse
     Ground with Parsley
½ teaspoon Lawry's Seasoned Salt
1 egg, slightly beaten
⅓ cup flour
2 cups bread crumbs

3 tablespoons olive oil
Salt and pepper

1. Place the pork loins in a reclosable freezer bag. (Be sure all the air is out of the bag before you zip it.) Wrap the bag loosely in an old bath towel (clean, of course). Place the package in the driveway behind the back wheels of your car. Depending on whether your car is compact, mid-size, or luxury, roll back and forth over the pork until it is approximately ¼ inch thick. Approximately 4 times for compact, 3 times for mid-size, and once for luxury. (Read the Epilogue before you try this.)

2. In a pie plate, mix the lemon juice, garlic, seasoned salt, and egg. In a separate pie plate, mix the flour and crumbs. Dip each pork loin in egg batter and then in crumb mixture. Repeat. Refrigerate until the rest of the meal is ready to serve.

3. In a large skillet, heat the olive oil on medium-high heat and quickly brown the pork loins (approximately 3 minutes on each side). Serve immediately.

Tips: If there is leftover crumb and egg mixture, mix them together, label, and freeze. The mixture can be used in casseroles, and is excellent added to our recipe for Potatoes Marengo (see Index).

Also, since the engines in most cars are in the front, use the front tires to smash thick cuts of meat, and the rear tires for thinner cuts.

Barbecued Pork Tenderloin Smoked over Applewood Coals

Don't let the applewood coals part scare you. Any kind of wood chips make barbecued pork tenderloin irresistible, but since we live in the state of Washington (where Johnny Appleseed must have hit the manic part of his career), we have easy access to the trees and, therefore, the chips. You can buy wood chips for barbecuing at stores where barbecue equipment is sold. Sears has a nice variety.

Soak the chips in water for about an hour before putting them on hot charcoals so they'll burn slowly and give whatever you are barbecuing the most flavorful smoke taste possible.

Sliced thinly, these make a delicious appetizer at parties, but they also make a scrumptious main course.

PREPARATION TIME: 5 minutes
MARINATING TIME: 30 minutes
COOKING TIME: 35 minutes
SERVES: 4

4 teaspoons Lawry's Garlic Powder Coarse
    Ground with Parsley
1 cup Bull's-Eye Original Barbecue Sauce
2 (1 pound) pork tenderloins
Salt and pepper

1. In a gallon-size reclosable freezer bag, mix the garlic and barbecue sauce. Put the pork in the bag and allow to marinate for 30 minutes.
2. Season with salt and pepper. Grill over hot coals for approximately 35 minutes, or until done.

Tip: Serve with Fighting Dragon Chinese Mustard (see Index) and a small shallow bowl of sesame seeds.

Sicilian Red Snapper Sub Rosa (Under Cover)

The Phony Gourmet should get an Oscar for this one. Starring red snapper, this fabulous dish works very well with its costar, Totino. Your family will love this so much they'll want it for dinner tomorrow night, too.

PREPARATION TIME: 7 minutes
COOKING TIME: 45 minutes
SERVES: 4

1 small onion, thinly sliced
1 tablespoon butter
1 tablespoon olive oil
1 (6-ounce) can tomato paste
¾ cup chicken stock
2 whole cloves garlic
1 teaspoon Lawry's Seasoned Salt
4 red snapper fillets
1 Totino's Three Meat Party Pizza
Salt and pepper

1. In a medium skillet, sauté the onion circles in butter and oil over medium-high heat until translucent (3 to 4 minutes).
2. In a blender, blend the tomato paste, chicken stock, garlic, and seasoned salt. Pour the mixture over the onions in the skillet; lower the heat and cook 5 minutes on medium-low. Season with salt and pepper.
3. Place the fish in the bottom of a buttered 11-inch deep-dish pie plate. Pour the contents of the skillet over the fish and top with upside down pizza. Cover with foil and bake in a 375-degree oven for 35 minutes. Remove the foil and bake another 10 minutes.

Chinook Salmon Steaks with Hollandaise

Nothing compares with fresh Chinook salmon from the northwest. Served with velvety-smooth hollandaise sauce, it is absolutely elegant.

PREPARATION TIME: 15 minutes
BAKING TIME: 12 to 13 minutes
SERVES: 4

4 (8-ounce) Chinook salmon steaks
¼ cup mayonnaise
2 tablespoons fresh lemon juice
½ teaspoon Lawry's Seasoned Salt
½ teaspoon Lawry's Garlic Powder Coarse Ground with Parsley

FOR THE SAUCE:
4 tablespoons (½ stick) butter
1 (0.9-ounce) package Knorr Hollandaise Sauce Mix
1 tablespoon Best Foods or Hellmann's Dijonnaise
1¼ cups milk

2 teaspoons fresh lemon juice
Chopped fresh parsley and green onions for
    garnish
Sliced lemon for garnish

1. Rinse and pat the salmon steaks dry with paper towels. Brush both sides with mayonnaise and drizzle with lemon juice. Sprinkle with seasonings.
2. Place the salmon steaks in a shallow baking dish sprayed with Pam.
3. Bake at 375 degrees for 6 to 7 minutes. Carefully turn and brush with the pan juices. Bake another 6 minutes.

For the sauce:
1. In a small saucepan, melt the butter over medium heat. Stir in the sauce mix until blended.
2. Remove from heat. Stir in the Dijonnaise and milk.
3. Stirring constantly, bring to a boil over medium-high heat. Reduce the heat and simmer, stirring, 1 minute. Stir in the lemon juice before serving.
4. Serve the salmon steaks with the sauce. Garnish with parsley, green onions, and lemon slices.

Good served with small red potatoes and a green salad.

Tips: Don't overcook the fish or it will be dry. If you can't get fresh salmon, frozen will do, but remember that any fish that has been frozen and thawed will have a drier texture than fresh. Halibut steaks may be substituted for salmon.

William Penne Pasta with Pesto

Our dad, Bill Young, loves pasta, but he's not a yuppie. He still calls it noodles. He doesn't care what shape it's in, he just loves it! We love it too, and we think that the different shapes are fun. We like to eat bow ties, small tubes, big tubes, grooved tubes, tiny radiators, coils, strands, ribbons, hats, pillows, slabs, half moons, conch shells, and butterflies. Still, we're talking about noodles. In case you didn't know it, the bow ties and the butterflies are called farfalle, the small tubes are called penne, the big tubes are called cannelloni, and the grooved tubes are rigatoni. Tiny pasta radiators are radiatori, the coils are either gemelli or rotelle, the half moons are mezzalune, and the conch shells are conchiglie. The strands and ribbons (depending on how wide they are) are either fedelini, fusilli, tagliatelle, tagliarini, pappardelle, or the more familiar Italian ribbon brothers, fettuccine, linguine, and spaghetti. The hats are tortellini, the pillows are ravioli, and the slabs are lasagna noodles. While Bill Young calls all pasta "noodles," and you can, too, don't be afraid to play with the shapes and pick your favorites. This recipe is one of our dad's favorites.

Diagonally cut at the ends, the penne pasta we used in this dish has a four-star restaurant look of elegance. The pesto sauce is fresh, light, and colorful.

PREPARATION TIME: 3 minutes
COOKING TIME: 10 minutes
SERVES: 4

4 quarts water
2 cups uncooked penne pasta

FOR THE SAUCE:
1 package Knorr Pesto Sauce Mix
½ teaspoon Lawry's Garlic Powder Coarse
    Ground with Parsley
3 tablespoons grated Parmesan cheese

1. In a large kettle, bring the water to a boil. Add the pasta and cook 8 to 10 minutes. Rinse and drain.

2. Follow the package directions for pesto sauce. Add the garlic powder.

3. Pour the sauce over the pasta and toss. Sprinkle with Parmesan cheese.

Tip: To serve as a main entrée, add 1½ cups diced, cooked chicken. If fancy people are going to eat with you and you think they subscribe to a gourmet magazine, chop up about 3 pieces of sun-dried tomatoes (3 tablespoons), throw in 2 tablespoons of pine nuts, and put a hardcover Martha Stewart cookbook on the coffee table.

Whoppers Under a Sheet

If you love a Whopper now and then, you will love this recipe. Pick up the burgers on your way home, throw out the sack, dismantle the burgers, and no one will ever guess what went into this delicious entrée.

PREPARATION TIME: 5 minutes
COOKING TIME: 20 minutes
SERVES: 4

2 Whoppers from Burger King
½ sheet Pepperidge Farm frozen Puff Pastry
    Sheets, thawed 20 minutes
½ cup chopped onion
1 tablespoon Bull's-Eye Barbecue Sauce
2 tablespoons catsup
1 tablespoon water
1 tablespoon Dijon-style mustard
½ cup grated Tillamook Cheddar Cheese or
    other Cheddar of your choice

1. Cut everything that was in between the buns of the Whoppers (lettuce, pickles, hamburger, and sauce) into bite-size pieces. (Use a long knife to scrap the buns clean.) Place in a greased medium-size casserole dish. Set buns aside.

2. In a cup or small mixing bowl, mix the onion, barbecue sauce, catsup, water, and mustard. Pour over the hamburgers. Sprinkle with the cheese.

3. On a floured board, roll the pastry into a size large enough to cover the Whopper mixture.

4. Bake in a 400-degree oven for 20 minutes.

Tip: Toast buns in oven (insides up) for 5 minutes before the Whoppers Under a Sheet are done. They are crispy, crunchy, and delicious additions to this meal.

EAT YOUR VEGETABLES

Baked Potato Salad Boats

All the great tastes you get in potato salad. This is truly a dinner in a potato. You can make these tasty potatoes ahead and refrigerate until ready to bake and serve.

PREPARATION TIME:
15 minutes
COOKING TIME:
1 hour, 30 minutes
SERVES: 4

4 large baking potatoes
1 cup chopped ham (optional)
1 cup shredded Tillamook Cheddar Cheese
   or other Cheddar of your choice
2 stalks celery, finely chopped
4 green onions, chopped
4 tablespoons (½ stick) butter or margarine, softened
½ cup Best Foods or Hellmann's
   Mayonnaise
½ cup sour cream
2 large kosher dill pickles, chopped
1 teaspoon Lawry's Seasoned Salt
½ teaspoon pepper

1. Prick and bake the potatoes at 425 degrees for 1 hour, or until tender on the inside.
2. Cut out a small section of skin lengthwise in each potato and scoop the pulp out into a large mixing bowl. Add the ham, cheese, celery, green onions, butter, mayonnaise, sour cream, pickles, seasoned salt, and pepper. Mix thoroughly.
3. Spoon the mixture back into the potato shells and bake for 30 minutes.

Back Burner Beans

With your choice of spices or herbs, you can make this bean dish travel all over the globe.

PREPARATION TIME: 4 minutes
COOKING TIME: 4 to 5 hours
SERVES: 8

2 cups dried beans (any kind)
5 cups water
1 teaspoon Lawry's Seasoned Salt

1. Rinse the beans.
2. In a 5-quart soup pot, cover the beans with the water and simmer on medium-low heat for 4 or 5 hours.
3. Decide which direction they will go by what kind of spices you add, in addition to the seasoned salt. If you want to take them to Mexico, add taco seasonings. If Italy is your destination, add spaghetti seasonings. For Germany, add dry mustard, dill, and a ham bone. Be creative.

Oktoberfest Potatoes

There won't be any leftovers with this zesty potato dish. Great served with Wiener Schnitzel Michelin.

PREPARATION TIME: 15 minutes
BAKING TIME: 25 minutes
SERVES: 6 to 8

7 *medium red-skinned potatoes*
½ *pound bacon, cut in 1-inch pieces*
1 *medium onion, chopped*
½ *cup vinegar*
2 *tablespoons cornstarch*
1 *cup water*
1 *teaspoon Lawry's Seasoned Salt*
½ *cup sugar*

1. In a large saucepan, boil the potatoes with their skins on for 20 minutes, or until tender. Drain, cool, and slice ¼ inch thick into a 2-quart casserole dish.
2. In a medium skillet, fry the bacon until browned. Drain on paper towels. Remove most of the drippings from the skillet.
3. Sauté the onion in the remaining bacon drippings over medium heat. Add the vinegar, cornstarch dissolved in water, seasoned salt, bacon, and sugar. Cook and stir over medium heat until thickened, 3 or 4 minutes. Pour the sauce over the potatoes and toss. Bake, covered, in a 350-degree oven for 25 minutes.

Potatoes Marengo

Remember, to us anything Marengo means use whatever you have on hand. This is a great make-ahead dish that kills two jobs with four potatoes. Feed the family, clean out the refrigerator.

PREPARATION TIME: 15 minutes
COOKING TIME: 1 hour, 30 minutes
SERVES: 4

4 *baking potatoes*
1 *tablespoon Crisco*
1 *teaspoon Lawry's Seasoned Salt*
1 *cup assorted vegetables on hand in the*
    refrigerator
½ *cup minced onion*
1 *cup grated cheese (use cheese that's close*
    to collecting Social Security)
¼ *cup (½ stick) butter or margarine, softened*
½ *cup sour cream*
1 *whole clove garlic*
Freshly ground pepper

1. Massage Crisco into the potatoes and sprinkle them with seasoned salt. Prick and bake at 425 degrees for 1 hour.
2. While the potatoes are baking, clean out the refrigerator and collect approximately 1 cup of vegetable odds and ends that aren't long for the crisper.
3. In a food processor, purée assorted vegetables, onion, cheese, butter, sour cream, garlic, and seasoned salt. Place in a large mixing bowl.
4. When the potatoes are done, cut them in half lengthwise and spoon out the pulp into the processed mixture. Mix well. Refill the potato shells and refrigerate until ½ hour before dinnertime.
5. Bake in a 400-degree oven for 30 minutes.

South-of-the-Border Homemade Refried Beans

From Pam

I love Rosarita Refried Beans, but one day I just happened to look at the label and was shocked to see that there was lard in them. I later discovered that Rosarita makes a delicious vegetarian version, free of lard, but the recipe I developed is so easy to make from scratch that I wanted to include it in this cookbook. It is also vegetarian, but it tastes every bit as good as Rosarita's lard-laced rendering. This bean recipe will make the equivalent of about 2 large cans of refried beans. It will freeze very well in reclosable freezer bags and is wonderful to use in any recipe requiring refried beans. Layer the beans with cheese, sour cream, chopped tomatoes, olives, green onions, jalapeños, and lettuce, and serve with sturdy tortilla chips.

For 5 minutes of effort, you'll have a month's supply of the best-tasting refried beans this side of the Rio Grande, AND your house will smell simply fabulous while they cook.

PREPARATION TIME: 5 minutes
SOAKING TIME: Overnight
COOKING TIME: 5 to 6 hours
MAKES: 5 cups

2 cups dried pinto beans
6 cups water
2 teaspoons chili powder

2 tablespoons plus 1 teaspoon Presti's Spicy
    Taco Seasoning (see Note)
1 large onion, quartered
4 whole cloves garlic
2 teaspoons dry mustard or 1 tablespoon
    Dijon-style mustard
1 tablespoon Lea & Perrins Worcestershire
    Sauce
1/2 teaspoon Tabasco sauce
Freshly ground pepper

1. In a 4- to 5-quart kettle, soak the beans overnight in cold water to cover.
2. In a food processor, combine the water, chili powder, 2 tablespoons taco seasoning, onion, garlic, mustard, Worcestershire sauce, Tabasco sauce, and ground pepper. Process until the onions are finely chopped. Store the spiced mixture in a covered container in the refrigerator overnight.
3. In the morning, drain and rinse the beans. (They claim the water that goes down the drain takes with it the culprit we hear and smell, but never speak about.) Add the refrigerated spice mixture to beans. Cover and simmer 5 to 6 hours on low heat, stirring every hour or so, until beans are very tender.
4. In a food processor, purée all but 1 cup of beans. Add the cup of unprocessed beans

(to give the mixture a nice texture) and the remaining 1 teaspoon taco seasoning.

Tips: This recipe will store for a week in the refrigerator, and up to 6 months in the freezer. Whenever a recipe calls for a can of refried beans, head for these.
    Long, slow cooking will give any bean recipe the fullest flavor.

Note: We buy Presti's Spicy Taco Seasoning at Costco (a wholesale outlet), in an 11-ounce jar. It has herbs, spices, garlic, onions, and salt and the pieces are so big that the mixture looks like potpourri.

Onion-Roasted Potatoes

Round out your meal to perfection with this excellent potato side dish.

PREPARATION TIME: 5 minutes
BAKING TIME: 40 minutes
SERVES: 8

1 packet Lipton Recipe Secrets Onion Soup
    Mix
2 pounds all-purpose baking potatoes, cut
    into large chunks

⅓ *cup olive oil*
Chopped fresh parsley and green onions for
garnish

1. Put the soup mix, potatoes, and oil in a large reclosable freezer bag. Close the bag and shake until the potatoes are evenly coated.

2. Empty the potatoes into a shallow baking dish; discard the bag. In a 450-degree oven, bake the potatoes for 40 minutes, stirring occasionally, or until the potatoes are tender and golden brown. Garnish with parsley and green onions.

Broccoli-Leek Quiche

Anytime you serve quiche, diners are impressed. Actually, anytime you serve anything in a crust, most people think you know something they don't. To this smarty-pants pie called "quiche," add leeks (which scare people in the grocery store anyway) and you walk away with the gourmet prize.

We buy rolled-out pie dough, ready to put in our own baking dishes, from a local restaurant we frequent. Famous for its pies, this restaurant hires experienced bakers who come in the middle of the night and make the pies while we sleep. They get the shells ready for us to pick up when we come in for breakfast. The only thing we have to remember to do is call the day before and leave our order with the manager so that the all-night bakers don't accidentally bake our crusts. Sometimes we have them get the whole pie ready to go into the oven. Then we bake it at home and transfer the homemade delight to our own pie plate before serving. If you don't happen to have a friendly baker, you can buy a frozen, unbaked pie shell at the supermarket, or make your own.

This fast, flavorful quiche is terrific as a light dinner entrée or a delicious meal in itself for brunch.

PREPARATION TIME: 15 minutes
COOKING TIME: 45 minutes
SERVES: 6

1   *package Knorr Leek Soup*
1   *(10-ounce) package frozen chopped*
      broccoli, thawed and well drained
1½ *cups shredded Cheddar cheese*

½ cup diced ham
¼ teaspoon pepper
1 (9-inch) unbaked pie shell
3 eggs
1½ cups half-and-half

1. In a large bowl, combine the soup mix, broccoli, cheese, ham, and pepper. Spoon into the pie shell.
2. In a medium bowl, beat the eggs and half-and-half until well blended. Pour over the mixture in the pie shell.
3. Bake in a 375-degree oven 40 to 45 minutes, or until a knife inserted 1 inch from the edge comes out clean. Let stand 10 minutes before serving.

Country Fair Grilled Walla Wallas

If you've ever been through the state of Washington in the summer, you've heard of our Walla Walla onions. As soon as they're in season, we buy them in 50-pound sacks. In our travels we've heard toutings about other sweet onions from other parts of the country, but of course we think ours are the best.

Torch up the barbecue and grill these sweet white giants, letting their wonderful aroma take you straight to the country fair on a warm summer day.

PREPARATION TIME: 5 minutes
GRILLING TIME: 15 minutes
SERVES: 6

3 Walla Walla sweet onions, cut in
    quarters vertically, then each quarter
    cut in half
1 tablespoon olive oil
½ teaspoon Lawry's Seasoned Salt
½ teaspoon Lawry's Garlic Powder Coarse
    Ground with Parsley
1 teaspoon Schilling Dill Weed

1. Place the onion pieces on a sheet of heavy aluminum foil that has been sprayed with Pam. Sprinkle the onions with oil and seasonings, wrap loosely, and shake the foil package gently to distribute seasonings evenly.
2. Open the foil and place the partially wrapped onions on top of the hot barbecue grill. Grill for 10 to 15 minutes.

Good served with everything!

Tip: Onions are best when grilled just until tender, but not transparent.

Walla Walla Bing Bangs

If you can get your hands on Walla Walla sweet onions, you must try this recipe! It's the stuff dreams are made of.

PREPARATION TIME: 15 minutes
COOKING TIME: 20 minutes
SERVES: 6

3 large Walla Walla onions (see Note),
     3 to 4 inches in diameter
1 (10-ounce) package frozen chopped
     broccoli, thawed and well drained
¾ cup grated Parmesan cheese, plus
     additional for topping
⅓ cup mayonnaise
2 tablespoons fresh lemon juice
2 tablespoons butter or
     margarine
2 tablespoons flour

¼ teaspoon salt
½ teaspoon Tabasco sauce
⅔ cup milk
1 (3-ounce) package Philadelphia Brand
     Cream Cheese, cubed
Chopped fresh parsley

1. Peel the onions, remove the tops and bottoms, and slice in half horizontally. Boil in salted water for 10 to 12 minutes; drain.
2. Leaving ¾ inch edges, remove the centers of the onions. Place onion shells in a shallow greased 1½-quart baking dish.
3. Chop the centers of the onions to equal 1 cup. Combine the chopped onions, broccoli, cheese, mayonnaise, and lemon juice. Spoon into the onion shells.
4. In a small saucepan, melt the butter; stir in the flour, salt, and Tabasco. Gradually add the milk. Cook until thick, stirring constantly. Remove from heat and blend in the cream cheese. Spoon the sauce over the onions. Bake at 375 for 20 minutes. Sprinkle with parsley and additional cheese.

Note: If you can't get Walla Walla onions, use the largest, sweetest onions your grocery can get. Texas Sweets are very good, as are vidalias.

Aunt Peg's Five-Bean Summit Meeting

From Peggy

I don't know what it is about men and baked beans, but they seem to go together like an ox and a cart. The next time you're at a buffet where baked beans are served as a side dish, observe how differently men and women approach the pot. Put a piping hot bean pot in front of a male and he'll dig in as if he's on a cattle drive and he's just heard the call, "Come and get it!" Women, on the other hand, are cautious with beans, even in the privacy of their own homes. In public, a lady might allow herself a taste, but a man has no shame when it comes to loading up his plate. "Just pile it on and let 'er rip!"

While this recipe comes from cans, it couldn't be duplicated commercially unless five major corporations merged. I marry the contents of my favorite cans of baked beans (diners can't identify any single brand so they assume I have baked them myself) and I doctor them up with my own touches.

I think my favorite compliment over the years came from my nephew, Michael. He said, "Aunt Peg, you make the absolute best baked beans in the world. How do you do it?" He's an attorney, so I was scared to tell him the secret, lest it be a violation of patents or something. Instead, I said I'd send him the recipe and then I didn't.

These baked beans are so delicious that I have passed them on as gifts. At bridal showers I give the bride-to-be an old-fashioned bean pot, a good manual can opener, and the recipe.

PREPARATION TIME: 10 minutes
BAKING TIME: 2 hours
SERVES: 10 machos or 50 prissies

1 medium onion, chopped
½ pound bacon, cut into pieces the size of a
    dime
½ teaspoon Lawry's Garlic Powder Coarse
    Ground with Parsley
1 (16-ounce) can Van Camp's Pork and
    Beans
1 (16-ounce) can Heinz Vegetarian Beans
    in Tomato Sauce
1 (16-ounce) can Campbell's Old
    Fashioned Baked Beans
1 (16-ounce) can S&W Premium Baked
    Beans with Brown Sugar
1 (28-ounce) can B&M Brick Oven Baked
    Beans (they're the base)
1 tablespoon Dijon-style
    mustard

4 hard shakes Lea & Perrins Worcestershire
    Sauce
1 packed tablespoon brown sugar
3 tablespoons Bull's-Eye Barbecue Sauce
½ cup cubed smoked ham (this is impres-
    sive)

1. In a skillet, sauté the onion, bacon, and garlic. Drain and set aside.
2. Into a large crockery cooker or bean pot, dump the 5 cans of beans.
3. Add the sautéed onion, bacon, and garlic. Doctor the bean mixture with mustard, Worcestershire sauce, brown sugar, barbecue sauce, and smoked ham.
4. Heat the conglomerate for a couple of hours on low (250 degrees) to make the beans look authentically slow-baked.

Tip: Get the empty cans out of the kitchen immediately!

NOW YOU CAN HAVE DESSERT

Mousse in Almost a Minute

In the time it takes to melt a candy bar, you will have a dessert your family will beg for.

PREPARATION TIME: 5 minutes
MELTING TIME: 5 minutes
SERVES: 8

*1 (7-ounce) Hershey's Symphony Creamy
    Milk Chocolate Candy Bar (plain)*
2 cups heavy cream, whipped

In a small saucepan, melt the chocolate over low heat. Gradually add melted chocolate to whipped cream. Eat.

Tip: Top with C. W. Crumb Crunch (see Index).

Bounce Off-the-Walls Popcorn Balls

These treats will be a hit at any kids' party. Or, if your children are listless or bored, just pad the walls and serve.

PREPARATION TIME: 10 minutes
COOKING TIME: 5 minutes
SETUP TIME: 10 to 15 minutes
MAKES: 2 large balls

½ cup (1 stick) butter
⅓ cup oil
1 pound miniature marshmallows
1 cup mixed nuts (optional)
1 (8- to 10-ounce) package Milk Duds
6 quarts unsalted popped corn

1. Melt together the butter, oil, and marshmallows.
2. In a large bowl, combine the nuts, Milk Duds, and popcorn. Pour the melted marshmallow mixture over all, mixing quickly and thoroughly. Press into 2 large buttered bowls. Let set up 10 to 15 minutes before popping out of bowls.

Tip: You'll want to be making that appointment for the children's semiannual dental exams.

Bundles of Joy

This elegant chocolate dessert is fun to serve, since you know that the secret ingredient is baby food. Of course no one can ever know that you robbed the cradle to get the delicate taste and texture that give the illusion of a carefully prepared French dessert.

PREPARATION TIME: 5 minutes
BAKING TIME: 20 minutes
SERVES: 4

4 Pepperidge Farm frozen Puff Pastry Shells
1 (7-ounce) Hershey's Symphony Creamy Milk Chocolate Almonds & Toffee Chips, melted and cooled slightly
1 cup heavy cream, whipped
1 (6-ounce) jar Gerber's Dutch Apple Dessert (3rd food variety)
C. W. Crumb Crunch (see Index)

1. On an ungreased cookie sheet, bake the pastry shells, unthawed, in a 400-

degree oven for 20 minutes. Cool. Take the top off each shell and hollow out the shells with a fork.

2. Fold the melted candy bar into the whipped cream. Spoon an equal amount of baby food into the bottom of each cooled pastry shell. Top with whipped topping mixture. Refrigerate.

3. Top with C. W. Crumb Crunch.

Vermont Maple Cream Tarts

From Pam

Terry's family comes from Vermont, the maple-sugar-oozing capital of the world. Because his uncle Herb still lives in New England, we get to go there more often than we would if nobody we loved lived there. Consequently, I have been blessed with a direct and sweet supply of maple syrup. (Terry won't allow the words "log cabin" to be spoken in our home.)

One Sunday morning while I was remoting, I landed on a cable channel where a woman was giving a recipe for maple cream pie. The show was called "Amish and Quilt Country" (or something like that). I was lured by the fact that the filling for this recipe had only TWO ingredients, and one was real maple syrup!

I have changed the recipe to make it even easier to prepare. When I took it to the family's annual Thanksgiving feast, I received more compliments for this dessert than I have ever had in my life.

Rich, rich, rich, but light, light, light at the same time! A taste treat that will start a tradition.

PREPARATION TIME: 10 minutes
COOKING TIME: 10 minutes for filling, 20 minutes for pastry shells
SERVES: 6

1 package Pepperidge Farm frozen Puff Pastry Shells, baked according to package directions
1 (14-ounce) can Eagle Brand Condensed Milk
¾ cup REAL maple syrup (no substitutes, please!)

FOR THE TOPPING:
¼ cup powdered sugar
1 teaspoon vanilla
1 pint heavy cream, whipped

½ cup chopped pecans
1 tablespoon butter

1. Bake the pastry shells in a 400-degree oven for 20 minutes. Cool. Take the tops off and hollow out the shells with a fork.
2. Over medium heat, slowly bring the condensed milk and syrup to a boil that can't be stirred down (about 10 minutes), and pour into the baked pastry shells. Chill.
3. To make the topping, gradually add the powdered sugar and vanilla to the whipped cream. Mound the topping into each shell until it overflows.
4. In a small saucepan, sauté the chopped pecans in butter over medium-high heat until browned. Be careful—they turn brown fast! Cool and sprinkle over each filled shell.

Tip: No substitutes for the heavy cream. If you are watching your weight, just have a bite or eat this only once a year.

Snickers Under a Blanket

No one will ever recognize that Mr. Snickers is the main character in this delicious dessert.

PREPARATION TIME: 5 minutes
COOKING TIME: 20 minutes
SERVES: 4

1 sheet Pepperidge Farm frozen Puff Pastry Sheets
2 (2.1-ounce) Snickers candy bars (see Note)
¼ teaspoon water

1. Thaw the pastry sheet for 20 minutes. Roll out on a floured board and cut two 7 × 4-inch rectangles.
2. Place each candy bar upside down in the middle of a pastry sheet. Wrap so that the pastry will be double on the bottom (They are going to bake upside down.) Seal by using ¼ teaspoon water along edges. To close ends, moisten well with water and use a fork to mash the ends closed. (If the Snickers aren't sealed tightly, there won't be much of a laugh when you have to scrape Mr. Snickers's cooked guts off the cookie sheet.)
3. Place each bundle on its seam on an ungreased cookie sheet. With a small knife, make 3 tiny vents (about ¼ inch) in the top of each bundle.
4. Bake in a 375-degree oven for 20 minutes. Cut each bundle in half to serve.

Great served with vanilla ice cream.

Note: You don't have to use Snickers candy bars. We just liked the sound of Snickers Under a Blanket. Actually your favorite candy bar will work just fine with this recipe. We've tried all the greats: Mounds, Butterfingers, Milky Ways, and, if you like BabyRuths you can call this BabyRuth in a Blanket.

Four Skor and Seventeen Pecan Pie

Using candy bars in desserts is like using bouillon cubes in soups and stews. The delicious flavor in a Skor candy bar is unbelievably exquisite in a pecan pie, and the candy bars take the place of at least 4 ingredients!

PREPARATION TIME: 5 minutes
COOKING TIME: 50 minutes
SERVES: 6 to 8

4 *eggs*
¼ cup (½ stick) butter, softened
5 (1.4-ounce) Hershey's Skor Candy Bars
    (4 for the pie, 1 for you to eat while you make it)
1 cup dark corn syrup

1 unbaked 9-inch pie crust
17 pecans (approximately 1 cup)

1. In a food processor, blend the eggs, butter, candy bars, and corn syrup until smooth.
2. Pour the egg mixture into the unbaked pie shell, add the pecans, and fold gently to make sure they get coated with the egg mixture.
3. Bake in a 400-degree oven for 50 minutes.

Strawberry Long Cake

Elegant, delicate, and unforgettably delicious.

PREPARATION TIME: 10 minutes
SERVES: 6

2 cups chilled heavy cream
1 (7-ounce) Hershey's Symphony Creamy Milk Chocolate Candy Bar (plain)
1 (12-ounce) Sara Lee Pound Cake, thawed
2 cups sliced fresh strawberries
1 cup C. W. Crumb Crunch (optional; see Index)

1. Whip the cream while melting the candy bar on low heat. Gradually add the melted candy bar to the whipped cream.

2. Cut the cake into two horizontal layers.

3. Frost between the layers and the top and sides of the cake with the whipped cream mixture.

4. Distribute the berries evenly over the top. Sprinkle the optional cup of crumbs on top of the berries.

Cotton-Tail Delight

From Peggy

Ally loves strawberries so much that she has her own strawberry patch. She gathers berries all summer long (they're everbearing plants) and it's always a race with the bunnies to see who gets to them first. Next to her strawberries, I have a patch of carrots, and we have discovered that Peter Rabbit chooses the berries over the carrots every time.

This yummy combination of pretzels, strawberries, crunch, and fluff is just incredible!

PREPARATION TIME: 10 minutes
BAKING TIME: 8 to 10 minutes
CHILLING TIME: 3 hours
SERVES: 8

2 cups crushed pretzels
¾ cup (1½ sticks) butter, melted
1 cup plus 3 tablespoons sugars
1 cup sugar plus 3 tablespoons sugar
1 (8-ounce) package Philadelphia Brand Cream Cheese, softened
1 (8-ounce) container Cool Whip
1 (6-ounce) package strawberry Jell-O
2 cups boiling water
1 (10-ounce) package frozen strawberries

1. In a small bowl, combine the crushed pretzels (see note), melted butter, and 3 tablespoons of the sugar. Press into a 9 × 13 pan. Bake in a 350-degree oven 8 to 10 minutes. Cool.

2. In the same bowl, mix together the remaining 1 cup sugar and the cream cheese until light and fluffy.

3. Fold in the Cool Whip.

4. Spread the mixture over the baked pretzel layer, touching all sides of the pan so that none of the pretzel layer shows.

5. Dissolve the Jell-O in the boiling water. Add the berries. Let set in refrigerator until thickened to the consistency of egg whites, but not firm. Pour over the cream cheese mixture. Chill.

Note: Place in a reclosable freezer bag and roll over the bag with the car. See Epilogue.

Apple Orchard Sticky Buns

Serve these gorgeous breakfast rolls warm, as a sweet addition to a special Sunday brunch.

PREPARATION TIME: 5 minutes
BAKING TIME: 20 to 25 minutes
SERVES: 10

¼ cup (½ stick) butter
½ cup brown sugar
½ cup chopped walnuts (optional)
1 cup canned apple pie filling
2 (11.5-ounce) cans refrigerated cinnamon rolls

1. In an 11-inch glass pie pan, melt the butter in a microwave oven. Add the brown sugar, nuts, and apple pie filling. Arrange the cinnamon rolls over the mixture, cinnamon side down, starting around the outside and overlapping the edges of each roll. (In this recipe, do not use the frosting that comes with the cinnamon rolls.)
2. Bake in a preheated 375-degree oven until golden brown.
3. Immediately and carefully invert onto a serving platter to remove the buns from the baking dish.

Tip: The frosting you didn't use can be spread on graham crackers as an after-school snack.

Caramel Apple Pie

This deliciously simple dessert is too good to be true. Make it for no reason and it will be something nobody will forget. Make it for a special occasion and it will become a tradition.

PREPARATION TIME: 15 minutes
BAKING TIME: 45 minutes
SERVES: 8

36 Kraft Caramels
2 tablespoons water
4 cups sliced green apples
¾ cup flour
⅓ cup sugar

1 teaspoon cinnamon
⅓ cup margarine

1. Place the caramels and water in a 9-inch glass pie plate. Microwave on medium setting about 3 minutes, or until the caramels melt. Add sliced apples. Stir to coat apples with melted caramel.
2. In a small mixing bowl, mix the flour, sugar, and cinnamon. Add the margarine and cut up with a fork or pastry blender until the mixture is the size of tiny peas.
3. Top the carameled apple slices with the strained mixture. Bake in a 375-degree oven 40 to 45 minutes.

Tip: After the first 10 minutes of baking (or whenever the topping has browned), put a loose piece of aluminum foil over the pie to prevent overbrowning. Make sure there is another rack above the rack the pie is on so that the foil doesn't touch the top element and short everything out.

Flopsy, Mopsy, and Cotton-Tail Pie

Pretend you're Mr. McGregor and guard this strawberry dessert against marauding nibblers who'd devour it behind your back. We don't know how to make this pie easier to cut for company, but everybody will eat it so fast that it won't matter!

PREPARATION TIME: 10 minutes
CHILLING TIME: 3 hours
SERVES: 8

1 (8-ounce) package Philadelphia Brand Cream Cheese, softened
⅓ cup sugar
1 cup Cool Whip
1 (9-ounce) graham cracker crust
4 cups hulled fresh strawberries
⅓ cup semisweet chocolate chips
2 teaspoons shortening

1. In a medium bowl, mix the cream cheese and sugar.
2. Fold in the Cool Whip and pour into the graham cracker pie shell.
3. Place the strawberries, point sides up, on the filling.

4. In a medium saucepan, melt the chocolate and shortening; drizzle over strawberries. Chill.

Mocha Angel Food Torte with Fresh Strawberries

If you were a stodgy old gourmet, you'd make this light, glorious torte the hard way. If you'd rather be a phony gourmet and get out of the kitchen fast with the same delicious results, you'll love this recipe!

PREPARATION TIME: 15 minutes
SERVES: 12

1   *package chocolate pudding*
1½ *tablespoons Taster's Choice Hazelnut (or any other flavor) Instant Coffee*
1⅓ *cups milk*
1   *cup Cool Whip*
1   *(10-inch) tube angel food cake from bakery*
15   *Almond Roca candies, crushed*
1   *pint fresh strawberries, sliced*

1. In a medium saucepan, combine the chocolate pudding and instant coffee. Cook the pudding following the package directions, but use only 1⅓ cups milk. Cool.
2. Beat the pudding mixture until smooth. Fold in half the Cool Whip. Split the cake into 3 layers. Spread half of the pudding mixture between the layers.
3. Fold the remaining ½ cup Cool Whip into the remaining pudding mixture. Use to frost the top and sides of the cake. Sprinkle crushed Almond Roca over the top of the cake. Chill until serving time. Just before serving, fill the tube of the cake with sliced fresh strawberries.

Tip: The Almond Roca candy can be put in a reclosable freezer bag and wrapped loosely in foil, then crushed by the weight of the car to save time. See Epilogue.

White Chocolate Camouflage Frosting

From Peggy

I gave my first wedding shower on May 1, 1994. My niece, Joanna, was the bride-to-be. I wanted everything to be perfect for her: the cake, the punch, the decorations, the games, and the prizes. The recipe I'm going to give you is for the cake, but first I'll tell you about the shower.

Joey's accent colors for her wedding were shades of purple and magenta. My entire yard sang a hallelujah chorus of colors for the prenuptial celebration. Just before the shower, I picked lilacs, lavender and shocking pink rhododendrons, red violet chrysanthemums, and purple pansies, and I put them everywhere. (My house smelled just like a funeral parlor!) I chilled the purple pansies in a bowl of cold water, and at the last minute I scattered them around the punch bowl on the table and I used them to decorate the glorious white chocolate cake that I'm going to tell about later. My living room looked as if Mother Nature was a houseguest.

I wanted the shower to be different from every other bridal shower I'd been to. Actually, I hadn't been to one since I was young and we played games like "try to drop the clothespin into the milk bottle." I guess that gives you an idea of how old I am, because they don't even make milk bottles anymore and I'm not sure what's available in the clothespin line. (My neighbor hangs sheets and stuff on her clothesline with something, but I don't know what it is.

I always admire it though.) Anyway, I wanted games nobody'd ever played before, so Pam and I made up some new ones.

The first game was "guess who you are." We made name tags and pinned them on the backs of each of the guests as they arrived. They were told that they were famous for one of three things: love, romance, or sex. It was a great ice-breaker, as guests who had been strangers asked yes or no questions of each other to figure out their identities. We had everyone from Rudolph Valentino, Jimmy Swaggart, and Pepe Le Pew to Lorena Bobbitt, Dr. Ruth, and Senators Packwood and Kennedy at the party. Anyone who guessed whose name was on their back got to pick from one of dozens of little grab-bag-type prizes I had in a pretty purple basket. It was fun to watch the guests turn into little children as they earned the right to paw through the basket of goodies I'd "gathered" from hotels I'd stayed in while traveling. The treasures consisted of toiletries like shower caps, shoe horns and polishes, sewing kits, lotions, shampoos and conditioners, mouthwashes, and soaps. Since every hotel tries to outdo the other, it was a lovely array of merchandise.

Another game we played also began at the front door as the guests arrived. Each one received a sheet of those fluorescent sticky dots (9 nickel-size dots to a sheet). They were told to put a dot on anyone who said any of the following words: Joey (or Joanna), Marc, the groom-to-be, wedding, or love. When they ran out of dots they got to dig into the prize basket again. Because I was preoccupied with all the details of hosting the party, I wasn't watching my mouth. I ended up covered with dots!

The last game was one of chance. The twenty guests sat in a circle around a coffee table piled high with prizes. I had twenty-five items (just in case someone came without RSVPing) all wrapped in the same hot pink paper and decorated with two tiny pink and purple rosebuds glue-gunned to them. I bought the flowers and paper at a craft supply store. The two little bunches of roses and the paper, sold by the foot, came to under four dollars. Heaped with the presents, the coffee table was a decoration in itself. (One of the first young ladies to arrive looked at the huge stack of gifts and said, "Wow, you really went all out for Joanna; I only got her one present!")

I explained to the guests that some of the packages contained booby prizes, while others were really quite nice! After telling everyone to pick one and take a seat in the circle, I gave Joanna a wicker tray with a pretty magenta bow on it and a pair of oversize dice.

The object of the game was to trade prizes with someone else, (hopefully upgrading) by rolling the dice on the tray and getting doubles or the equivalent of seven or eleven. The dice went around the circle once before each guest opened the package she had. Then I set the timer for an undisclosed number of minutes (it was ten) and the tray kept going around the circle. I had purposely bought some real dogs, like deodorant and garbage bags, but there were a couple of really nice ones like a wicker picnic basket with plates, cups, and eating utensils, and a small insulated cooler that everyone wanted. The average prize was in the two- to three-dollar range (bath beads, a box of candy, dishcloths, panty hose, and the like). I bought only items that would wrap easily. The picnic basket, of course, was the biggest prize. As the clock ticked on, the basket and the cooler changed hands many times. As the dice would have it, just as the timer went off, someone threw doubles and snatched the wicker right off the lap of the lady next to her. Stripped of the coveted container, the loser walked away with a box of cotton balls.

With the games over, I asked Joanna to

lead everyone to the refreshments so she could get her punch and cake and start opening her presents. (A friend made a wedding rehearsal bouquet for her, using all the ribbons and bows from the gifts and a paper plate for the base.) The cake table was really pretty! I'd made an ice heart with purple pansies frozen inside to float on top of the punch. The mold was one of those plastic hearts sold by Hallmark. I put the pansies facedown in the bottom of the heart and weighted them down with clean dimes. Then I covered the pansies with water and put the mold in the freezer. Before the heart was completely frozen, I removed the dimes.

The cake I served was a spinoff of a white chocolate masterpiece I found in a southern magazine. When I saw it, I knew I had to have it for Joanna! It was decorated with edible violets and the writer said that making the recipe was truly a labor of love. You had to bake the cake, make the frosting, and crystallize the flowers. With a couple of months before the shower, I could picture myself pulling it off from scratch, but as the day grew closer and my time grew shorter, I had to face reality. I love Joey, but even without the frosting and the crystallized violets, the recipe for the cake alone had nine ingredients and four paragraphs of instructions! I didn't have that much time to spend laboring over a cake, so out of love I bought one naked and spent the time I had making my own frosting.

I have no problem with bakery cakes; it's the frosting that I don't like. It coats the roof of my mouth. Two days before the shower, I ordered a white sheet cake from the bakery and asked them to price it without frosting, filling, or decorations. It was a request they'd never had before, but they came up with a price of $6.99 for half a sheet. I brought it home and frosted it with my own white chocolate camouflage and nobody suspected that the cake itself was off the rack.

This bridal shower indulgence marries the best of two families: the perfect cake that is the backbone of your favorite bakery and the pure, irresistible, rich frosting you make at home.

PREPARATION TIME: 10 minutes
COOKING TIME: 10 minutes
SERVES: 25 people (½ sheet cake)

2 (8-ounce) packages Philadelphia Brand
    Cream Cheese
2 (3-ounce) packages Philadelphia Brand
    Cream Cheese

⅔ cup butter
1 (12-ounce) package best-quality white
      chocolate chips
12 cups sifted powdered sugar
3 tablespoons vanilla extract

1. Let the cream cheese and butter soften at room temperature for about an hour.
2. In a heavy saucepan, melt the white chocolate chips over low heat, stirring constantly. Remove from the heat and cool 10 minutes, stirring occasionally.
3. Beat the cream cheese and butter at medium speed with an electric mixer until creamy. Gradually add the cooled white chocolate, beating constantly until blended. Gradually add powdered sugar and vanilla, beating until smooth.

Tip: Instead of sifting the powdered sugar, put it in a food processor—it will be finer. Decorate the frosted cake at the last minute with edible pansies that have been chilled in cold water. They don't need to be crystallized; in fact they are prettier plain and they taste like sweet wild clover.

Tip: R.S.V.P. means that the favor of a reply is requested. In other words, pick up the phone and make the call.

Variation: Use light margarine and light cream cheese if it makes you feel better, but with 12 cups of sugar, who are you kidding? Besides, a wedding shower is not an everyday event!

Georgia Peachy Bars

These peachy bars would be good enough for Scarlett O'Hara to eat at a barbecue at Twelve Oaks!

PREPARATION TIME: 10 minutes
BAKING TIME: 25 minutes
MAKES: 36

1 (8-ounce) can Pillsbury Crescent Dinner
      Rolls
1 cup chopped pecans
⅓ cup sugar
½ teaspoon cinnamon
¼ teaspoon nutmeg
6 peaches, peeled, halved, and puréed

FOR THE TOPPING:
1 cup shredded coconut
½ cup flour
½ cup firmly packed brown sugar
¼ cup chopped pecans
¼ cup (½ stick) margarine

1. Separate the dough into 2 long rectangles.

2. Place the rectangles in an ungreased 9 × 13-inch baking dish and press together to form a crust.

3. In a medium bowl, combine the pecans, sugar, cinnamon, and nutmeg. Sprinkle over the crust.

4. Spoon the sliced peaches evenly over the nut mixture.

5. In the same bowl, mix together the topping ingredients until crumbly. Sprinkle the topping over the peaches.

6. Bake in a preheated 375-degree oven for 25 minutes, or until golden brown. Cool completely. Cut into 36 bars.

THIS AND THAT

Fighting Dragon Hot Chinese Mustard

We had just returned from Wok-King, a Chinese restaurant, and we were discussing the subject of stir-frying, agreeing on how quick and easy it is to do. It was obvious that my sister was distressed about something.

"What's the matter, Sissy?"
"Oh, nothing. I've just got some pork in my teeth."
"Good lunch, huh?"
"Yeah."
"Where's your doggy bag?"
"Oh, shoot. I left it in the restroom."
"That's better than leaving it in the car. Last summer I left a couple of crab legs in the station wagon, and every cat in the neighborhood was in the driveway."

"Whatever happened to that car? Did you ever get the smell out?"
"Nope. We sold it to a guy at the beach."

"You wanna take a class in Chinese cooking over at the college with me?"

"Oh, I don't know. Who teaches it this quarter?"

"Mel Davis."

"Spare me. Has he been to China?"

"No, but he fought in the Korean conflict and he came back loaded with recipes."

"Do the Chinese cook the same as the Koreans do?"

"I don't know. Just sign up with me."

"Doesn't Mel Davis teach painting on velvet?"

"Yeah. I'm telling you, Sissy. He's really been everywhere. He even spent some time in Mexico."

"Yeah, I know. I've seen his bumper stickers."

"Don't judge a man's cooking ability by his bumper stickers. Do you want to go with me or not?"

"No!"

"No?"

"No. I'm happy with what I've learned from the chef at the Fighting Dragon."

Hot, but so good for barbecued Chinese pork or anything you want to dip into a little excitement.

PREPARATION TIME: 4 minutes
MAKES: ⅓ cup dipping sauce

1 tablespoon dry mustard
½ teaspoon salt
½ teaspoon cayenne pepper
2 teaspoons vinegar
½ cup light cream

In a small bowl, blend the seasonings with the vinegar, mixing until smooth. Add the cream.

C. W. Crumb Crunch

This buttery, nutty crumb topping is great sprinkled on ice cream or over any dessert with a whipped cream topping. It will add flavor, crunch, and a smile to anyone who has teeth.

PREPARATION TIME: 4 minutes
COOKING TIME: 3 minutes
MAKES: 1 cup crumbs

1 cup C.W. Post granola cereal
1 tablespoon butter

In a small skillet, melt the butter over medium-high heat. Sauté granola in the butter until browned.

The Incredible Crouton

From Pam

I have been making my incredible croutons for at least twenty years. Originally, I developed the recipe because I didn't want to throw away a stale loaf of bread. As the word got out and noses from all over the neighborhood sniffed out the crunchy culinary cubes, I found myself actually shopping for outdated loaves to turn into after-school treats and television snacks. Many a stuffed guest has lumbered out of my front door after dinner with a mayonnaise jar of croutons in one hand and the secret recipe in the other. Now, at last, you too can create crouton magic in your own kitchen.

The savory aroma of garlic bread will waft through your entire house for hours.

PREPARATION TIME: 15 minutes
COOKING TIME: 3 hours
MAKES: Approximately 625 croutons or 2½ quarts

1 loaf of cheap (3 or 4 loaves for a dollar)
*   white bread at least 3 days old, crusts*
*   left on*
1 stick butter or margarine (left out until it's
*   as warm as the kitchen)*
1 teaspoon Lawry's Garlic Powder Coarse
*   Ground with Parsley*
2 teaspoons onion powder
2 teaspoons Lawry's Seasoned Salt

1. Butter (or margarine) each slice of the bread on one side and restack the loaf.

2. Cut through half the loaf at a time, lengthwise and widthwise, to end up with lots of little ¾-inch squares. Dump the cuttings (don't worry about separating them because they'll fall apart in the oven) onto a large cookie sheet. Sprinkle on the seasonings.

3. Toast in a 250-degree oven for up to 3 hours, tossing throughout the toasting process whenever you think of it.

Fat-Free Plus Mayonnaise

From Pam

I have been going to Weight Watchers for years, and I have narrowed my "width factor" to just a couple of things. One of the culprits is my affair with mayonnaise. Like an expert who knows fine antiques from antique replicas from Taiwan (circa 1995), I consider myself a connoisseur of the divine spread. So, when I left Weight Watchers one day with the injunction to eat fat-free mayonnaise (Kraft Free to be exact), I was depressed.

I would never have believed that I would actually LOVE the stuff, but I do. It's only because I have added my own touch of spices and ingredients, because the taste, for me, was off a hair or two. (Sorry for that analogy.) The texture is exactly like real mayonnaise, so all I needed to work on was the taste. I came up with a recipe that makes it taste even BETTER than the real thing, and it's fabulous when used in potato salad, great mixed in tuna, and, when it is smeared on bread for a turkey sandwich, only a psychic would be able to know the truth.

It's a miracle. Invest in Kraft!

PREPARATION TIME: 5 minutes
MAKES: 1 quart

1 quart Kraft Free Mayonnaise
2 tablespoons rice vinegar
3 tablespoons lemon juice
1 teaspoon Lawry's Garlic Powder Coarse
   Ground with Parsley
Fresh ground pepper

1. In a medium mixing bowl, combine all the ingredients.
2. Put back in the jar and use as needed.

Tip: Use whenever mayonnaise is needed in a recipe. Try it in your next baked potato or as a dip for artichoke leaves.

Molly McMelt

Nothing can beat the taste of real butter, but it's also one of the culprits for putting those extra pounds and inches on stomachs and cheeks (both kinds). Molly McButter can't beat the taste of real butter, but somebody over at Alberto-Culver had a nice set of taste buds when he/she tasted this product into existence. If you are watching your weight, 1 tablespoon of butter is 100 calories and 1 tablespoon of Molly McMelt is 5 calories.

Use this delicious, buttery substitute for real melted butter and before you know it, you'll be back into that pair of unzippable jeans you have stashed in the back of the closet.

PREPARATION TIME: 2 minutes
COOKING TIME: 1¾ minutes
MAKES: 1 cup

1 cup water
4 tablespoons Molly McButter
2 teaspoons cornstarch

1. In a small microwave-safe bowl, whisk together 1 cup water and two teaspoons cornstarch. Microwave for 1¾ minutes until bubbly, stirring once.
2. Whisk in 4 tablespoons of Molly McButter until dissolved. Refrigerate up to 3 days.

Tip: When a recipe says to melt butter or margarine in a skillet and sauté meats or vegetables in the melted butter or margarine, substitute chicken, beef, or vegetable stock for the measurement of butter or margarine. Sauté as the recipe directs, and afterward add the Molly McMelt. Reduce the amount of seasoned salt or salt, because there is a lot of salt in Molly McButter.

Ripoff Italian Tomato Sauce

Double this recipe and store in the refrigerator for a week. It tastes better as the days go on. It's great to use as a spaghetti sauce.

PREPARATION TIME: 3 minutes
MAKES: about 2 cups

1 (15-ounce) can or jar of anybody's tomato
    sauce (choose your favorite)
1 teaspoon Lawry's Garlic Powder Coarse
    Ground with Parsley
1 tablespoon Italian seasoning

Open the can and add the garlic and Italian seasoning, using the can or jar as a mixing bowl. Mix and use as needed. Store in a glass jar with a tight-fitting lid.

Phony Gourmet Gourmet Sauce

Delicious with green beans, peas, and spinach.

PREPARATION TIME: 5 minutes
COOKING TIME: 5 minutes
MAKES: 2 cups

1 cup milk
1 (8-ounce) package Philadelphia Brand
    Cream Cheese
1/2 cup shredded Parmesan cheese

In a small saucepan, heat the milk and cream cheese until the cream cheese is melted. Stir in the shredded Parmesan, and continue stirring until it melts.

Basic Ripoff White Sauce

White sauce like Grandmother used to make, except for the Lawry's.

PREPARATION TIME: 5 minutes
COOKING TIME: 5 minutes
MAKES: 2½ cups

1/4 cup (1/2 stick) butter or margarine
1/4 cup flour
2 cups milk
1/2 teaspoon Lawry's Seasoned Salt

1. In a small saucepan, melt the butter over medium-high heat.
2. When the butter starts to bubble, reduce the heat to medium and add the flour, stirring for 3 minutes. (It will look as if you are frying the flour, which is what you are doing. But don't let it brown.)
3. Add the milk and seasoned salt and cook until the sauce thickens and starts to bubble.

Tip: Add ½ cup of the cheese of your choice for great cheese sauce to cheese up vegetables.

Crispy, Crumby, Counterfeit Cover-up

Use this delicious crumb topping on casseroles or as a crispy coating for baked fish or chicken. Other uses are suggested throughout the book.

PREPARATION TIME: 10 minutes
MAKES: Enough crumbs to hide approximately 12 meals

3   *cups dry Potato Buds*
3   *cups plain Progresso Bread Crumbs*
1½ *cups mixed nuts*
2   *teaspoons Lawry's Seasoned Salt*
2   *teaspoons Lawry's Garlic
       Powder Coarse Ground with Parsley*
2   *teaspoons onion powder*
½   *cup olive oil*

1. In a food processor, process the instant potatoes, bread crumbs, nuts, seasoned salt, garlic powder, and onion powder.

Gradually add the olive oil and continue processing until well blended.
2. Freeze in a large reclosable freezer bag. Use when you need to hide something.

Tip: To make a cheese topping, add an equal part of grated cheese of your choice to the recipe.

Twice-Baked Bread

Make any loaf of uncut bakery bread look like something that just came out of YOUR oven!

PREPARATION TIME: 3 minutes
COOKING TIME: 9 minutes
MAKES: 1 loaf

1 loaf unsliced bakery bread
2 tablespoons flour

1. Spray a light mist of Pam on top of the loaf of bread, followed by a generous dusting of flour.
2. Wrap the bread in aluminum foil and bake in a 400-degree oven for 6 minutes.
3. Uncover and continue baking for 3 minutes longer.

Dilly of a Fish Sauce

Unlike a more pungent tartar sauce, this mild yet flavorful sauce brings out the best in any grilled fish.

PREPARATION TIME: 5 minutes
CHILLING TIME: 1 hour
MAKES: about 1 cup

2 tablespoons margarine, melted
1 cup sour cream
1 tablespoon Schilling Dill Weed
1/8 teaspoon white pepper

In a small bowl, mix the margarine, sour cream, dill, and pepper. Chill 1 hour.

EPILOGUE

From Jeff (Peggy's son)

When I first picked up this book in manuscript form, it was to look for comma splices and misspelled words—not because I enjoy squandering what little free time I have away from school on learning how to make Skinny Hawaiian Chicken à l'Orange. No, I've always been much simpler in my culinary nature than that. Since I have had my own apartment, for the first time I have been forced into the kitchen to concoct my own meals.

The solution? Ramen. Cases of it. Of course, every time I go home (which is often because I'm starving) my mom and dad load me up on prefab food from Costco. Unfortunately, about $200 worth of food only lasts about 3 weeks when I get back to school, and then it's back to my four creative renditions of ramen noodles: with the broth, without the broth, or either way with lots of salt.

So, when ending run-on sentences and fixing my mom's and my aunt's grammar began to make me hungry, I decided to try one of the recipes. The victim: "Wiener Schnitzel Michelin." I liked this one, not because of any affinity for pork, but because I liked the idea of serving Vicki, my fiancée, and saying, "Oh, it's just something I ran over today."

I called my mom with the good news that I was going to try one of her recipes, and then I walked across the street to Safeway to buy the stuff I needed (because I was fresh out of everything except ramen). As my stomach growled I put the pork in a "reclosable freezer storage bag," wrapped it "loosely" in foil, since I didn't have a clean towel handy, and grabbed my keys.

The meat was a pretty thick cut (but then how would I know?), so I opted for the front tires, where the weight of the engine would neatly compress my dinner to exactly ¼-inch thick. LESSON #1: Do not, under any circumstances, try to compress meat under the wheels of a car that is parked on an incline. I put my share of the meat just behind the front tire of my Honda Civic (the car was headed downhill), hopped in, and fired 'er up. With all four cylinders screaming with at least two horsepower apiece, I casually put it into reverse and let off the parking brake. The car, which I had only had for two weeks, began to roll down the incline, away from the pork, toward the car parallel-parked in front of me. I gave it (much) more gas and let out the clutch. The front tires spun right over the meat and shot it forward about four feet into the back end of the other car. I scraped the kill off the guy's bumper and threw the corpse of my mutilated meal into the Dumpster. Determined to prepare an edible meal safely, I grabbed Vicki's former share of the meat.

Now, as my mom said in this book I'm no numskull. When there's a flaw in something I'm doing, like shooting pork at other people's cars, I make a change. This time I moved the car to a level area of the parking lot by my building (and I even cleared away the larger bits of gravel). I hopped into my little windup rocket, popped it into reverse, and slowly backed over the pork a few times. Satisfied, I turned off the car (to give the hamsters under the hood a rest) and jumped out to inspect my work. The pork looked exactly the same as it had before I ran over it, except for a perfect imprint of my tire in the foil.

By this time, the little guy who lives in my stomach was telling the little guy who lives in my head either to cook the pork as it was or head for the ramen. The little guy in my head won out by pointing out that I could easily smash the meat with Vicki's Jeep.

I picked up the pork and turned to the Jeep (which was already on level ground). I held up the recalcitrant pork so it could see its fate: a large, steel American monster with tires that could wade through 3 feet of wet cement (I imagine). I slapped the meat down on the pavement and climbed up into the cab. With a turn of the key, the monster roared to life, making my Honda seem a little sissyish (I always tell people it's hers and the Jeep's mine). But this time I didn't have to tell anyone anything: Now I was a real man in a real man's machine—a machine whose massive engine could drown out the sound of a jet—a machine that brings us to LESSON #2: Do not, under any circumstances, try to run over something you intend to eat with a vehicle that weighs over 5,000 pounds and has tire tread that looks like a tractor's. The meat was almost indistinguishable, save the fact that a stupid plastic bag and some bits of foil were mixed in with the remains. After making sure that nobody had been watching, I quickly scraped up the leftovers and ran into the house.

By this time, Head Guy was catatonic and Stomach Guy was getting really mad, but he was unprepared to deal with Mr. Ego, who promptly formulated LESSON #3: Never quit, even after things get pathetic, because if you can't even make a recipe from a phony gourmet cookbook, you will have to admit to yourself that you have some real problems.

I snatched up my wallet, locked the door, and headed back to Safeway. Feeling like a regular, I stepped up to the meat counter and picked out two more nice-looking pork tenderloins. When I got back to my building, my hands clammy with the feeling that I was going to either ruin the meat again or hurt myself this time, I walked right past my apartment to my friend next door.

Ken, the friend and owner of the mid-size vehicle I intended to borrow, happens to be much more technically oriented than I am. So, when I explained why I needed his car, he gave me one of those accusative "you stupid liberal arts major" looks and disgustedly handed me the keys. When I finished with the pork, it was uniformly ¼ inch thick (and treadfree) and ready for the skillet.

The rest of the recipe was surprisingly easy, mostly because the directions were much more precise. Frankly, I blame my mom and my aunt for their lack of consideration of the inherent hazards of the automotive portion of the preparation of this dish. I had intended to write them an anonymous letter of complaint, but when I saw how much Vicki loved the final result, I changed my mind. As she walked in the door, I was just placing the succulent, slightly browned pork on the table next to two ice-filled glasses of Kool-Aid. The look on her face wasn't the usual "what a lousy day at work—oh boy, he made noodles again" look. Instead, she looked both elated and baffled, like someone who had just won the lottery but hadn't bought a ticket. Confused and impressed, she thought that I had turned over a new leaf. She even called her mother and told her I was going to do the cooking from then on because I was so great.

Which brings us to LESSON #4: If you use this cookbook, the people you cook for won't let you off the hook anymore when you just come up with a dumb look and ramen noodles. They'll know that you somehow acquired the capacity to make the kind of food their mothers used to make, and they won't want anything less (but then again, neither will you).

From Pam and Peggy

When we were children on our way to some place special in the family car, we were often cleaned (almost like kittens) by our mother. As Dad pulled out of the drive-way, Mom would invariably spot dirt on one of us and, with a funny look in her eye, produce a hanky from somewhere. Short of licking us, she'd touch the hanky to her tongue and come after one of us, dabbing at some child-induced smudge. That's when she'd bring up what "they" would think. "What would they think if they saw you all dressed up with a dirty face?" We grew up wanting "them," whoever "they" were, to approve. "Always wear nice under-wear in case you have an accident and they have to take you to Vancouver Memorial where they will see it."

When we became adults, we knew it wasn't supposed to matter what anybody thought, yet we licked our kids, worried about their underwear, made sure they were well dressed, and today, we still clean for company, and love the idea of entertain-ing with a flair. Like it or not, we are still concerned with what "they" think.

It has occurred to us that there's a dif-ference between trying to impress some-one and trying to please. We've learned that we are not ever going to impress our families, because they already know everything about us. That leaves us with a purer notion, the desire to please. We hope you use this book in the spirit in which it was written. We hope it makes you laugh, gives you more freedom in your kitchen, and inspires you to please the people you love.

Our kitchens haven't changed very much over the last twenty years, but our lives certainly have. We no longer have lit-tle ones with sticky fingers and hungry after-school tummies making strikes at our refrigerators. There aren't any high-chairs (except for the one that comes when Laura, our first grandchild, gets to visit). There are no more pigtails or letter-person sweaters, fights over who ate the last piece of pie, or the cracking voices of male adolescents asking, "What's for din-ner?" The face of the refrigerator doesn't remind anyone to be at choir practice, soccer games, ballet lessons, or tae kwon do. Now they're magnetless and information-free. The cupboards don't showcase the colossal assortment of kid cereals they used to, and the counters aren't laden with lunch boxes, homework, or memos from teachers.

It's fun to think that if our kitchens could see, they would have seen everything that has ever happened to us over the years; and if they could talk, they could tell all. They would be able to tell about our plans and dreams, our failures, and our disappointments. Our kitchens would be able to tell what our kids wanted for Christmas every year, recite the Pledge of Allegiance in Spanish, name all the presidents, relay all the gossip that was exchanged in them, tell all the secrets and what went on in them when we weren't looking, like sneaking off diets and who knows what else.

If our kitchens could write, this is what we think they would tell other kitchens:

From Pam's and Peggy's Kitchens

Dear Kitchen,

You are the wisest of all the rooms in the house. You carry most of the memories, because that's where all the people in your house end up spending most of their time. The one who does most of the cooking may get frustrated once in a while, and take it out banging pots and pans around in front of you, but before he or she knows it the kids will be grown and out on their own and you'll get an R and R (Rest and Remodel).

We hope you will be able to collect as many happy memories as we have. God bless your sinks, counters, floor, oven, refrigerator, cupboards, drawers, appliances, cookware, gadgets, and God knows what else you hold. Most of all, God bless what you mean to your home and family.

Love,
Pam's and Peggy's Kitchens

INDEX